REES HOWELLS INTERCESSOR

STUDY GUIDE

MINA KOHLHAFER

PUBLICATIONS
Fort Washington, PA 19034

Rees Howells, Intercessor Study Guide
Published by CLC Publications

U.S.A.
P.O. Box 1449, Fort Washington, PA 19034

UNITED KINGDOM
CLC International (UK)
Unit 5, Glendale Avenue, Sandycroft, Flintshire, CH5 2QP

This printing 2020

Printed in the United States of America

ISBN (paperback): 978-1-61958-286-6
ISBN (e-book): 978-1-61958-287-3

Italics in Scripture quotations are the emphasis of the author.

Cover by Mitch Bolton.

Contents

REES HOWELLS, INTERCESSOR

For Use Individually or in a Group

How to Use This Workbook

Studying as an Individual

You don't have to be a Bible scholar to understand and be blessed by the Word of God or a spiritual biography like this. You just have to be willing to allow the Holy Spirit to be your teacher.

If you'll be studying this book on your own, follow these guidelines:

1. Set up a daily or weekly time to do this study. Begin with prayer and fellowship with God, then read the recommended chapters and complete the workbook pages.
2. Look up all the Bible verses as you come to them and meditate on each one.
3. As you go through each chapter in the workbook, focus your attention on the paragraphs to be read aloud.
4. Write out your answers to the questions.
5. When there is a Discussion or Personal Question, give the answer out loud so you can be blessed as you hear the answer.

6. Do each assignment as it comes up, so that the Lord will be able to point out the areas in your life that need to be changed.

Studying as a Group

1. Before each group meeting, read the designated chapters so that you can have an overall view of the chapters and be ready to participate.
2. Be sure to read the specified sections out loud. As you hear the truth of God's Word or of His dealings with Rees Howells, it is able to penetrate your heart and bring you to that blessed position where great and mighty revelations can enter in. Take the time to reflect on each "Read aloud" section, and discuss your thoughts with the group.
3. Fill in the blanks and answer questions with the group, as each specific area is discussed.
4. Complete the assignments at the end of each chapter at home by yourself. By doing this, you will allow the Holy Spirit to speak to you during the week and bring those things to your attention that need changing.

As a Quick Review Manual

When in need of a spiritual uplift, or a quick assist in getting back into the power place of God, thumb through the workbook and read the pull quotes (or, the quotes that are set apart from the rest of the text in this book).

Suggested Reading/Study Guide for Sixteen Weeks

Helpful Suggestions
for the Leader

You don't have to be a Bible scholar or a trained Bible teacher for God to use you mightily as a Bible study leader. You just have to be willing, and to acknowledge the Holy Spirit as the teacher.

> "Not by might, nor by power, but by my Spirit,
> says the LORD of hosts."
> —Zechariah 4:6

1. This workbook is based on the English Standard Version (ESV), but we suggest using many versions as you read, and that you identify them before reading.
2. Start with prayer, and as you get to know the members of the group call on various ones of them to pray.
3. If desired, allow a time at the beginning for one or two very short testimonies of what happened during the week to point out a truth from the lesson.
4. As leader, read the informative and instructive parts of the workbook aloud and see that everyone takes a turn reading the Bible verses and selections from the book, and answering the questions.
5. After you read aloud a section from the book, be sure to ask questions and encourage discussion.

6. Direct the Discussion and Personal Questions to the whole group. To get more response you might ask a specific person: "What do you think?" or "How would you do it?"

7. Especially emphasize the pull quotes that are throughout the workbook.

8. At the end of each group meeting, specify which chapters are to be read at home next (see suggested chapter reading guide) and remind them which assignments are to be done for the next meeting.

9. Go over the previous lesson's assignments at the start of the new session. Call on one or two students for their assignment answers, and give yours last as a summary.

Introduction

When the Lord first spoke to me to teach a Bible study on prayer, and use the book *Rees Howells, Intercessor* as my guide, I was not an intercessor. I didn't even know what the word *intercessor* meant. I never expected to be an intercessor, as I thought to be one you had to be somebody special. Moses, Joshua, Daniel, Jesus, and Paul were all intercessors (see Exod. 32:9–14; Josh. 7:6–10; Dan. 9:1–23; John 17:1–26; Col. 1:9–12). Yes, they were special, but all of God's children are special. All that was available to them is also available to you.

> The Lord God has given me
> > the tongue of those who are taught,
> that I may know how to sustain with a word
> > him who is weary.
> Morning by morning he awakens;
> > he awakens my ear
> > to hear as those who are taught.
> The Lord God has opened my ear,
> > and I was not rebellious;
> > I turned not backward.
>
> > > > (Isa. 50:4–5)

God loves you and wants you to walk in health and happiness. As you faithfully come into His presence daily for worship, fellowship, and guidance, a miraculous change will occur in your heart and mind. The energy of eternity and the resurrecting power of Jesus will come, making you in thought and deed and prayer-power more like Jesus.

Now, you are the one being taught! You are the one whose ears are being opened! You are the one who is obedient, I trust, and you are the one who is going to reach the throne of God for those in need! I am becoming the intercessor God is seeking—and so shall you.

—Mina Kohlhafer

Foreword

Prayer: *Heavenly Father, in the name of Your Son Jesus, pour Your light into our souls, and don't let us waver regarding Your promises, but strengthen our faith. Let us be transformed into His likeness more and more each day, and let Your glory shine through. Thank You, Lord.*

This verse sums up Rees Howells' life: "No unbelief made him waver concerning the promise of God, but he grew strong in his faith as he gave glory to God" (Rom. 4:20).

This verse can pertain to each one of us: "And we all, with unveiled face, beholding the glory of the Lord, are being transformed into the same image from one degree of glory to another. For this comes from the Lord who is the Spirit" (2 Cor. 3:18).

1. The foreword describes Rees Howells as one who is "beyond measure large-hearted." Who enlarges our hearts and sets them free?

_____

_____

Read First Kings 3:5–14; Psalm 119:32.

Discussion Question: Why do you need a spiritually enlarged heart?

Read aloud:

> "I remember one young Christian asking him how he knew God's voice, and he said, 'Can't you tell your mother's voice from any other?'
>
> "'Yes, of course,' the young man answered.
>
> "'Well, I know His voice just like that.'"

Hearing the voice of God is foremost in walking in the operation of the gifts of the Spirit, but more especially in intercessory prayer made under the Spirit's guidance. You should be able to discern God's voice from all others.

God spoke to Adam, Noah, Abraham, Moses, Joshua, Samuel, Elijah, Isaiah, Ezekiel, Peter, James, John, Paul, and many others. Read Exodus 33:9; Numbers 7:89; John 10:4–5, 27–28.

Personal Question: Are you one of these sheep, described in the aforementioned passages in John?

Personal Question: Can you also expect to hear God's voice?

You can hear and be guided by God's voice.

2. Read Psalm 46:10. What do you have to do to know God?

_____

_____

_____

3. Read Proverbs 8:34.
   Complete:

a. "_____ is the one who listens to me."

b. I am told to _____and to _____.

4. Read Psalm 32:8. List four things God says He will do for you.

a. _____

b. _____

c. _____

d. _____

5. Read Isaiah 58:11.

a. Rewrite this verse, inserting your name in appropriate places.

_____

_____

_____

_____

b. List some of the qualities of water, especially spring water.

_____

_____

_____

_____

Discussion Question: What does it mean *for you* to be like a well-watered garden, like a spring whose waters never fail?

This is the kind of relationship that is available to you when you listen to God—taking time to be still and quiet, and making yourself available to hear what He has to say, and most important, being obedient.

Chapter 1: Early Years

Rees Howells was born in 1879, in South Wales. Wales is the smallest of Great Britain's three countries. It is bounded on the east by England, and is made up of beautiful, harsh mountains, lonely uplands, coastal plains, deep lush valleys, coal-mining, and industrial areas. Its main cities are Cardiff and Swansea.

1. What two things are preeminent in the Howells' family life?

a. _____

b. _____

Discussion Question: What would happen in our nation if these things were also preeminent in the majority of homes?

2. List some of the dramatic changes that would take place.

_____

_____

_____

_____

Personal Question: How would it affect your home?

Read aloud:

> Even the normal pleasures of the world had no attraction
> for him. He would walk miles to hear someone preach and
> bring him "under the influence of God," but he "wouldn't
> cross the road to hear a concert." Only once did he even
> attend a football match. As the crowd were "shouting and
> bawling" around him, he felt it was not the place for him
> and vowed that, when he got his feet out of it, he would
> never go to such a place again. He never did.

Discussion Question: How do you stay under God's influence?

Discussion Question: Read First Corinthians 2:9–10. What
do these verses mean to you?

Personal Question: What can you foresee God bringing forth
in you?

Assignment

Write a prayer for your nation on "Godliness and love . . . in
the home." Try to use this in your daily prayers.

_____

_____

_____

_____

_____

Chapter 2: Two Shocks

"And until there is a conviction of need, there can never be a desire for a change. But God has *His* ways!" Consider this sentence in relation to all the people you want to see saved. Pray and believe.

Discussion Question: Discuss the "Hound of Heaven" poem. God has His ways of dealing with each individual. What are some of the ways God has worked in your life to bring about a conviction of need?

Read aloud:

> "I saw it!" said Rees. "I believed in the Savior, but one thing I knew, I wasn't *born* of Him. So far as having correspondence with the spiritual realm where the Savior lived, I was a dead man; I was outside the Kingdom, which all my good life and religion had never enabled me to enter. I was outside, though I was not a drunkard or a thief, because I had no correspondence with God."

1. What frequency and quality of correspondence do you have with God?

_____

_____

Personal Question: What can you do today to improve this correspondence?

If you are not born again, ask Jesus to forgive your sins and take control of your life right now—and correspondence will begin!

2. What is available to you from God? Read Psalm 25:5; John 16:13; First Corinthians 2:7, 10.

_____

_____

_____

_____

_____

Assignment

Write a prayer for an individual who is in need of knowing God, but doesn't have a desire to change.

_____

_____

_____

_____

Now, write a prayer for yourself, for God to show you how to deal with this person.

_____

_____

_____

Chapter 3:
Meeting the Risen Lord

Read aloud:

> He seemed to lose himself, and a vision of Calvary appeared to him. He said he witnessed every stage of the crucifixion. He forgot his own sufferings in the sufferings of the Savior, and as he gazed on the cross, the Master Himself said to him, "And must I bear the cross alone, and all the world go free?" From a broken heart Reuben answered, "No. There's a cross for everyone, and there's a cross for me."
>
> From that hour he was a new man. Instead of complaining at being in the asylum, he began to pray for the other twenty-nine, and to the Savior he said, "Let me suffer for You. Whatever You allow me to go through, I will never complain again."

1. Which will avail you more: prayer or complaining? Why?

_____

_____

_____

_____

Remember this the next time you are in a bad situation: Pray for the people enmeshed in it, rather than complain, and the Holy Spirit will change the circumstances!

2. In the story of Maurice Reuben, circle the two things that stand out in his relationship to God.

uneasiness   total obedience   kindness   hearing God's voice

Read aloud Rees' story of "what followed in that little Methodist chapel."

Can you say with Rees Howells: "The Savior became everything to me"?

3. List the qualities of a truly born-again person. Read Second Corinthians 5:17–20; First John 2:2.

_____

_____

_____

_____

_____

4. Look up the word *reconcile*.

_____

_____

_____

_____

_____

"I changed altogether. . . . The veil was taken back, my eyes were opened, and I *saw* Him." Read the following verses and you will also see and hear Jesus: Luke 1:30–33; 2:10–11, 40; 3:21–22; 4:1, 17–21.

Jesus' offices of Prophet, Priest, and King originated on earth, but continue in heaven.

Jesus is our *Prophet* as He communicates God's will and discloses the future to God's children. Read Deuteronomy 18:15–20; Matthew 13:57.

Jesus is our *Great High Priest* and *Intercessor* and draws near to the Father to plead on behalf of men. Read and discuss Hebrews 4:14–16; 7:22–25; John 17:7–9.

Jesus is our soon-coming *King*. Read Revelation 17:14; Zechariah 14:9.

> "When you receive the Savior, you receive the
> love of God."

Read aloud:

> "I saw that by His coming in to me, He would love sinners through me, as He loved me. It would not be forcing myself to love others, any more than the Savior forced Himself to love me. No person could be an enemy to me, because I had been an enemy to Him before I was reconciled. If I live in the realm where He is, I live to have mercy, to be kind and to love others. Could the love of God in me do harm to anyone? I had left the world and its folly and been born into that kingdom where there is only the love of God—the most attractive life on the face of the earth."

Personal Question: Is Jesus loving sinners through you?

Discussion Question: Why does Rees leave his job and return home?

Personal Question: What has claims on your time?

Time well spent—being mindful of the needs of others, always handling the situation as Jesus would—this is putting God first.

Assignment

Check the things that would not be a priority to God for your time.
( ) Watching inappropriate television
( ) Pulling weeds while praying in the Spirit
( ) Taking a thorn out of a child's foot
( ) Reading the Bible
( ) Spending unprofitable time on your phone
( ) Grumbling as you do the laundry
( ) Praising as you do the laundry
( ) Dwelling on bitterness all day
( ) Praying for the nation as you clean or cut the lawn
( ) Washing dishes while praying
( ) Taking out the garbage while praying for your neighbor
( ) Reading novels that do not glorify God
( ) Meditating on the Word

In all instances, be led by the Holy Spirit, and be a doer of the Word!

Chapter 4: The Welsh Revival

1. What are the two hindrances to blessing, found in the beginning paragraphs of this chapter?

a. _____

_____

b. _____

_____

Read John 14:23; Luke 6:37.

Personal Question: What are the main hindrances in your life that keep God's blessings from overtaking you?

Obedience to the promptings of the Spirit and open confession of Christ brought down the blessing. Jesus forgives instantly—and so should we!

Nothing should offend us when we are walking in the love of God. Don't let the devil get your mind and cause you to use up God's valuable time by dwelling on vain imaginations, resentments or other bitterness. Don't dwell on any unlovely thoughts. Read Psalm 119:165 (KJV).

Read aloud:

> The Revival proved what the Holy Spirit could do through a company of believers who were of one spirit and of one mind as on the day of Pentecost. The church had seen over and over again what the Lord could do through a yielded evangelist or pastor, such as Dwight L. Moody or Charles G. Finney, but in the Welsh Revival it was a divine power manifested through the church. The key note was, "Bend the church and save the world."
>
> The one aim was the saving of souls. The Savior said there is joy among the angels over one sinner that repents (see Luke 15:10), and they could say there was joy in the church over the converts. The bells of heaven rang every time, and there was a shout of victory in the camp.

Read aloud Acts 2:1; 8:5–8 (KJV).

2. What is to be the main aim in all we are doing?

_____

"The intercession of the Holy Spirit for the saints in this present evil world must be made through believers filled with the Holy Spirit."

Discussion Question: Rees says, "We felt the lack of power for service." What do you think he means by this?

3. Read Acts 1:8. Where does the power come from?

_____

_____

4. Read Acts 1:5; 5:32.

Complete: God gives His Holy Spirit to those who _____
Him.

Assignment

Look at someone who is filled mightily with the Holy Spirit, and describe what God does through him or her as a yielded, obedient vessel.

_____

_____

_____

_____

_____

Personal Question: Would you like God to work through you in this way?

What two things that we discussed above will you have to walk in?

1. _____

_____

2. _____

_____

Chapter 5: The Holy Spirit Takes Possession

"As Rees listened, he said to himself, *I know I am predestined according to the foreknowledge of God, and justified—but am I glorified?*" Read Romans 8:30; John 12:23–28.

Look up the word *glorified* in a Bible dictionary and discuss what it means.

Personal Question: Consider what you do in your personal life that does not glorify God. What can you do to change it?

To be glorified now is to be rid of self and continually partaking of the Divine nature, in constant communion with the Father so that the manifestation of God's power is flowing through one at all times. Read First Corinthians 10:31; John 17:21–23.

Read aloud the story of Rev. Evan Hopkins. Read Ephesians 2:1–6; First Corinthians 6:19; Romans 12:1.

"There is a place for you."

Discussion Question: Do you see a present aspect of glorification as Rees did?

Read aloud:

> "He made it very plain that He would never share my life.
> I saw the honor He gave me in offering to indwell me, but
> there were many things very dear to me, and I knew He
> wouldn't keep one of them. The change He would make
> was very clear. It meant every bit of my fallen nature was
> to go to the cross, and He would bring in His own life
> and His own nature."

1. What two things does the Holy Spirit bring in when you allow Him to?

a. _____

b. _____

Discussion Question: What wondrous things could be wrought in our families, cities, and nation if these two powers were at work within us?

Read aloud:

> "Like Isaiah, I saw the holiness of God. Seeing Him, I saw
> my own corrupt nature. It wasn't sins that I saw, but nature
> touched by the Fall. I was corrupt to the core. I knew I had
> to be cleansed; I saw there was as much difference between
> the Holy Spirit and myself as between light and darkness."

Prayer for cleansing: *In the Name of Jesus, we ask that You cleanse our hearts and open our minds to the light of Your Word. Deliver us from self and fill us with Your Holy Spirit.*

"[The Holy Spirit exposed] the root of my nature which was self. . . . Sin was canceled, and it wasn't sin He was dealing with; it was self."

2. What is "sin"?

_____

_____

_____

3. What is "self"?

_____

_____

_____

Personal Question: How can self be exposed and gotten rid of?

For the results of turning your life over to the Holy Spirit, read Second Peter 1:4 in the Living Bible and the New International Version.

Then comes the process of sanctification. "Step by step [the Holy Spirit] replaced the self-nature with His own divine nature."

4. Look up the word *sanctify*.

_____

_____

_____

5. Look up Psalm 51:10 (KJV), and write it here to use as a
   daily prayer.

_____

_____

_____

_____

_____

Read aloud:

> By Friday night, each point had been faced. He knew
> exactly what he was offered: the choice between temporal
> and eternal gain. The Spirit summed the issue up for him:
> "On no account will I allow you to cherish a single thought
> of self, and the life I will live in you will be 100 percent for
> others. You will never be able to save yourself, any more
> than the Savior could when He was on earth. Now, are
> you willing?" Rees was to give a final answer.

6. Look up the word *temporal*.

_____

_____

7. What does the Holy Spirit remind Rees must go for Him
   to come in?

_____

Personal Question: Can you say with Rees, "Lord, I am
willing"?

8. List what dynamic things happen when the third person of the Godhead comes in.

a. _____

_____

b. _____

_____

c. _____

_____

d. _____

_____

9. How can you better exalt the Savior in your daily life?

_____

_____

_____

_____

_____

Discussion Question: How has God's love worked in your life, and how can it work in the lives of those you are praying for?

Personal Question: That same Holy Spirit who entered the apostles on the day of Pentecost had entered Rees. Can God do this for you?

Streams of living waters flow out of those in whom the Spirit dwells. Read John 7:37–39.

Assignment

We have been talking about being *sanctified*, or meeting the qualifications for the *royal priesthood*. Read First Peter 2:9; Deuteronomy 7:6.

List the duties of the Old Testament priests.

_____

_____

_____

_____

_____

List the duties that compare, as you function in the office of a Holy Spirit-filled priest.

_____

_____

_____

_____

_____

Chapter 6: Loving an Outcast

1. What two objectives has the new divine Owner?

a. _____

b. _____

2. Look up the word *cultivate*.

_____

_____

3. Look up the word *fruitful*.

_____

_____

Discussion Question: How do these definitions compare to what God has been doing in your life?

4. We are like a potentially beautiful garden, but can only produce fruit after being carefully cultivated so that the weeds are all removed. List some of the things you might call weeds in your life.

_____

_____

_____

Effectual prayer must be guided praying.

"When the Holy Spirit comes in, He brings in the love of the Savior." Read John 3:16; 15:13; First Corinthians 13:4–7; Colossians 3:12–14.

Discussion Question: Rees learns that "he was never again to ask God to answer a prayer through others if He could answer it through him." How could this apply to everyday circumstances?

After Rees learns this important lesson, there are two situations where the Holy Spirit prays though him. He must obey the Scriptures in a very practical sense. Read aloud the story of Will Battery.

5. What might the Lord have you do in your household in order to let Him know you trust Him?

_____

_____

_____

> "If you love one, you can love many; and if
> many, you can love all."

The second time the Holy Spirit prays through him is for Jim Stakes. Read aloud the full story of Rees Howells giving Jim Stakes seventy pounds for his rent.

6. Complete:

"It was a conflict between _____ and

_____ for _____."

Personal Question: Can you look at each person, whether bad or good, and see him or her as a precious soul?

Discussion Question: When has the "joy of heaven" come down on you for obeying the Holy Spirit?

Personal Question: After Rees' "princely gift," Jim's wife is convicted as well. Love had conquered! Situations aren't changed by criticisms or sharp words—only by the love of Jesus radiating from you. Do you walk in this kind of love?

Prayer: *Lord Jesus, help me to walk in Your love and to show it forth to all I meet, especially those in my family.*

Read aloud:

> He continued his prayer-work for some eight hours a day, but with this difference: up to the time when the Holy Spirit took full possession, any need that arose automatically became a subject of prayer. But from henceforward, as with Rees, it was guided praying with specific objectives, victorious travail and definite answers.

7. List the three items of guided praying.

a. _____

b. _____

c. _____

Assignment

As the Lord brings people to mind that need prayer for salvation, list them here. Pray for these people with those three things in mind—and expect an answer!

Date   Name   *Date & Type of Answer*

_____

_____

_____

_____

_____

Chapter 7:
A Village Untouched by the Revival

Discussion Question: What does it mean to be a good shepherd?

1. "The Holy Spirit was going there, and He had authority to cast out devils and forgive sins." How does the Holy Spirit get into a situation?

_____

_____

_____

Read John 14:12; Mark 16:17–18.

2. Complete:

These young people "were coming with something _____

_____."

Discussion Question: How can we "live out the Bible" to people?

3. Complete:

"When he saw the_____ like that,
he was touched on a vital spot and _____."

4. What breaks bondages?

_____

_____

_____

> "'Cut the ropes and take the promises.' . . . 'The
> Holy Spirit showed me that if God wanted me
> to go anywhere, He would surely provide the
> means.'"

5. We can never really be "bondservants" until God does control our means. Rees recalls, "What joy I had in finding that I had finished with the limited resources of man and begun on the unlimited resources of God! The promises of God had replaced money in the bank and became equal to current coin to me. I no longer had to carry my treasure with me wherever I went because I knew where the treasury was, and how to reach it!" He trusts the Lord and "receive[d] a hundredfold now in this time" (Mark 10:30, KJV). Do you believe this can still happen? Why or why not?

_____

_____

6. Complete:

a. "His extremity was indeed God's _____."

b. "He had a claim on God's resources to_____

_____."

> **"What joy I had in finding that I had finished
> with the limited resources of man and begun on
> the unlimited resources of God!"**

Assignment

Find two promises in the Bible that are better than "money in the bank."

1. _____

_____

2. _____

_____

Chapter 8: The Tramps

God calls Rees to a day of prayer and fasting. When midday comes he is on his knees in his bedroom, but there is no prayer that next hour. "I didn't know such a lust was in me. . . . My agitation was the proof of the grip it had on me." Rees disobeys the Holy Spirit and goes to lunch. He comes face-to-face with disobedience to the Holy Spirit. To some people there might seem nothing in it, but once you are God's channel, on no account can you disobey Him or bring in your own ideas.

Discussion Question: Why should we not get ahead of God or use our own ideas?

Read aloud:

> He didn't take dinner for many days after that, but spent the hour with God. As he said later, "The moment I got victory in it, it wasn't a very big thing to do; it was merely a stepping-stone to His next call to me. It is while you still want a thing that you can't get your mind off it. When you have risen above it, He may give it back to you; but then you are out of its grip."

Discussion Question: What stands out in this paragraph?

Personal Question: How can you apply it to your own life?

Read aloud:

> [The Lord] laid on him the burden of the tramps—the many men who were to be found in that district wandering homeless and jobless from place to place. He and his coworkers were to give a chance to every tramp that came to the mission. It was to be a practical lesson of what divine love is towards an undeserving sinner. . . .

> "I soon found out also that the aim of the Spirit in this was to bring me to that grade in life where I would love the unlovely ones."

1. Read First John 4:7–21, and in your Bible circle all the times the word *love* is mentioned. What is the main thought of these verses?

_____

_____

_____

"Love the unlovely ones."

2. Why is God so strong in His command that we love all people?

_____

_____

_____

"The identification of the intercessor with the ones for whom he prays" requires feeling as they feel and sitting where they sit.

3. Read aloud Rev. Evan Hopkin's shipwreck illustration. Write a summary of how you personally have come through each of the three positions, and where you are now.

a. Struggling

_____

_____

_____

b. Clinging

_____

_____

_____

c. Resting (see Heb. 4:9–11; Isa. 30:15)

_____

_____

_____

> **"There were many disappointments; but some were allowed to disappoint us because it was part of our training."**

Assignment

List some of the disappointments of your life that turned into valuable lessons.

_____

_____

_____

Chapter 9: Binding the Strongman

1. While returning from the village one night, Rees and his friends pass a group of women who had been drinking. What does the Spirit tell Rees to do for the ringleader of those women—"a notorious character and a confirmed drunkard"?

_____

_____

_____

2. Complete:

"The Lord told him he was to use no _____

_____, but to reach her by way of

_____."

Read Matthew 12:29; John 15:7 (KJV and NIV).

3. Look up the word *abiding*.

_____

_____

4. "The scriptural key to abiding is in 1 John 2:6, 'Whoever says he abides in him ought to walk in the same way in which he walked.' In other words, it meant being willing for the Holy Spirit to live through him the life the Savior would have lived if He had been in his place." Write what this verse means in your own words.

_____

_____

_____

_____

_____

"The promise is unlimited, but its fulfillment depends on the abiding."

5. How does Mr. Howells maintain this abiding? Write down your answer, then read this section aloud.

_____

_____

6. What does the Holy Spirit then do in response?

_____

_____

7. Read John 15:5–8, 10; First Peter 1:22.

a. Where does the power come from?

_____

b. What can you do without Jesus?

_____

c. What has to remain in us to get our wishes?

_____

d. What gives glory to God?

_____

> **"As the intercessor remains united to Him by abiding in Him, His power operates through the intercessor and accomplishes what needs to be done."**

8. As Rees continues in the place of abiding, what does he become conscious of?

_____

Read aloud:

> "He began to deal with my nature," he said, "and show me things I never dreamed were there, getting deep down to my motives. It was a daily dying. Over and over again I thought: Is it possible to retreat?"

> But with obedience came cleansing, until by the second week, he said, "I had become more used to my position, and could see the Holy Spirit binding the devil. I soon realized I was not fighting against flesh and blood, but 'against wicked spirits in heavenly places.'"

Discussion Question: What does daily dying mean?

9. Read Ephesians 6:12. Who is our adversary?

_____

10. Read John 12:31–32. Who is going to be driven out of this world?

_____

11. Read Romans 16:20. Whom will God crush under our feet?

_____

12. Read Revelation 20:10. What is the devil's doom?

_____

13. Read Second Chronicles 32:7–8. Who is your great unseen power?

_____

Discussion Question: Consider Rees' prayer for the woman to come into the kingdom by Christmas Day. Could you pray for a desperate situation, totally by way of God's throne, and not in any way by hand or mouth try to influence it?

14. Complete:

a. "It was now a case of _____ before the victory."

b. "The Holy Spirit did not allow him to pray for her. . . . 'It would have been a _____ of _____.'"

Discussion Question: What does it mean to pray a "prayer of doubt"?

15. Look up Zechariah 4:6 and write the key portion here:

_____

_____

_____

Memorize this and know it is always by God's Spirit that things of God are brought forth!

Read aloud Rees' encounter with the woman with tuberculosis.

Discussion Question: "The Lord did more in a few minutes through their obedience than might have been done in hours without it." What things have happened to you when you were obedient to the Spirit's leading?

Assignment

Look up the word *obedience* in a Bible concordance, and see how many times it is used. Then pick out two of the most dynamic verses that show the power of obedience and write them down here.

1. _____

_____

_____

_____

_____

2. _____

_____

_____

_____

_____

_____

Chapter 10: A Branch in the Vine

Discussion Question: Why does the text say the Spirit was grieved? How do you grieve the Spirit?

Personal Question: The Holy Spirit says to Rees, "You are a branch in the Savior. The branch gets nothing—it is the needy that get the fruit. But after tonight, from this place of abiding, whatever the Father wants to pour out to the world through you, He can do so." Are you coming into that position where God can flow through you into the needy?

Discussion Question: Rees receives a letter from Mr. Gosset, offering to give him money should he ever need it for his work. All Rees would have to do is let him know, and Mr. Gosset would be happy to share. Norman Grubb writes, "That, of course, Mr. Howells would never do; *his needs were to be made known only by way of the Throne*." How would that command affect your life?

Read aloud:

> "It was a great joy in those days to think that the Savior had made me a branch—just a channel through which His own resurrection life could flow to the needy world. There is no closer relationship than between a branch and the Vine.

"But one thing the Husbandman cannot do is to graft the old life into the Vine. Self can never abide in the Savior—not one atom of it. Before you can be grafted into the Vine, you must be cut off from the old life. That had been going on and there were many stages in my life before this came. Without His new life, all our activity and work is, in the sight of God, as nothing. Yet the Vine can't do anything without the branch. All the sap of the Tree is running through the branch. And when this new life flows through us, every bit of us tingles with it, even our very body itself. If the Vine has joy, the branch has the same joy, and the needy get the fruit."

1. Complete:

a. "There is no closer relationship than between a

_____ and the _____."

b. _____ am the branch and _____ is the vine (see John 15:5).

2. Who gets the fruit you produce?

_____

_____

Discussion Question: Read Second Corinthians 5:17 (TLB and NIV). How is God accomplishing this in your life?

Assignment

In the block, illustrate your relationship to Jesus. Draw a vine and label it Jesus. Make it thick and full of sap, which is the power of the Holy Spirit. Draw a branch coming out to one side, which is you, receiving the sap. Draw a fruit on the end of your branch, which came from the power in the vine; and below, reaching up, draw a needy person.

When you look at this, remember that the only way the needy can get fruit from Jesus is when you are a functioning branch, flowing with power from the energy source.

Chapter 11: The Tubercular Woman

A woman in the village develops tuberculosis, and her doctor expects her to die. One evening, however, the Lord tells her that she will be healed. The next day she asks Rees if the Lord revealed anything to him about her healing. Rees tells her that He hadn't, "for up to that time the Holy Spirit had never given him any prayers for healing."

1. What kind of prayers had he been praying up to this time?

_____

_____

_____

2. For how long is Rees in daily prayer for this woman?

_____

"She was living on prayer."

3. This prayer necessitated:

a. A daily _____

b. A daily _____

c. A daily _____

Discussion Question: What does it mean to "go through"?

4. Read Matthew 8:16–17. Why should there not be freedom from the power and dominion of sickness?

_____

_____

_____

> **"The Holy Spirit can only make intercession through those human temples He indwells."**

Discussion Question: As an intercessor, a person must enter into the sufferings and take the place of the one prayed for. Have you ever been in this position? How have you handled it?

Read aloud the story of what happens after Rees runs two miles to the sick woman's house.

5. "The room was filled with His glory." What are the circumstances that allow the glory of God to fill that room?

_____

_____

_____

Read aloud:

"Before our dear sister passed away, she had left a message for me. 'Tell Rees and the others that I can't wait for them. The Savior has come for me, and I want to go with Him. Tell them I will come back to meet them' (see 1 Thess. 4:14). Then she had said good-bye, shaken hands all around, and had gone to be with the Lord. That glorious testimony of the first of the mission to sleep in Jesus made this 'failure' the sweetest thing in the world. . . .

"The sad grave was turned to be the gate of heaven, and from that funeral we had the beginning of resurrection life in the mission."

Discussion Question: How can a funeral be the beginning of resurrection life?

Discussion Question: Why was it necessary for the Holy Spirit to take the case?

Assignment

Write out what this means to you: "The first case of healing, the firstfruits of this intercession, belonged to the Lord and had to go to the altar."

_____

_____

_____

_____

_____

Chapter 12: What Is an Intercessor?

1. What central truth does the Holy Spirit gradually reveal to Mr. Howells?

_____

2. What two things does the Spirit constantly lead him into?

a. _____

b. _____

"God seeks intercessors but seldom finds them."

Read Isaiah 59:16; Ezekiel 22:30.

3. What are the three things to be seen in an intercessor that are not necessarily found in ordinary prayer?

a. _____

b. _____

c. _____

Jesus is our Divine Intercessor interceding for a lost world (see Heb. 7:25). God provided our Intercessor. Now He expects us to intercede for others who are unable to *identify* with Jesus, or are not interested in the *agony*, or are unequipped with the *authority*.

Identification is the first law of the intercessor. He pleads effectively because he gives his life for those he pleads for; he is their genuine representative; he has submerged his self-interest in their needs and sufferings, and as far as possible has literally taken their place.

Agony is to be found present only in the Holy Spirit, as Intercessor on earth, and He can work only through those whose hearts are His dwelling place.

"Self" has to go to the cross to be released from itself, in order to become the agent of the Holy Spirit. It is no theoretical death but a real crucifixion with Christ, with a "new man" coming to live on this earth!

Read Galatians 2:20.

Read aloud:

> As crucifixion proceeds, intercession begins. By inner burdens and by calls to outward obediences, the Spirit begins to live His own life of love and sacrifice for a lost world through His cleansed channel.

> We see it in Rees Howells' life. We see it at its greatest height in the Scriptures. Watch Moses, the young intercessor, leaving the palace by free choice to identify himself with his slave-brothers and sisters. See him accompanying them through "the howling waste of the

wilderness" (Deut. 32:10). See him reach the very summit of intercession when the wrath of God was upon them for their idolatry and their destruction was imminent.

It is not his body he now offers for them as intercessor but his immortal soul: "If you will forgive their sin—but if not, please blot me out of your book that you have written" (Exod. 32:32); and he actually called this "[making] atonement" for them (32:30).

4. What do you think is the most dynamic part of this set of paragraphs?

_____

_____

_____

5. List some of the concerns for others you know you should have, but don't yet have.

_____

_____

_____

6. What is the root of this unconcern?

_____

_____

_____

Discussion Question: How can this be overcome?

7. "Intercession is more than the Spirit sharing His groaning with us and living His life of sacrifice for the world through us. *It is the Spirit gaining His ends of abundant grace*." Look up the word *grace*.

_____

_____

Discussion Question: "If the intercessor knows identification and agony, he or she also knows authority. It is the law of the grain of wheat and the harvest." How can this law give you authority? Read John 12:21–26.

8. "There has only ever been one substitute for a world of sinners: Jesus the Son of God. But intercession so identifies intercessors with sufferers that it gives them a prevailing place with God." Look up the word *prevailing*.

_____

_____

Read aloud:

> Thus Moses, by intercession, became the savior of Israel and prevented their destruction; and we can have little doubt that Paul's supreme act of intercession for God's chosen people resulted in the great revelation given him at that time of worldwide evangelization and the final salvation of Israel (see Rom. 10–11), and is enabling God to bring it about.

9. What is the most dynamic portion of this paragraph?

_____

_____

_____

10. Rees often talks about the "gained position of intercession." Write out the four steps and read the associated
verses. Discuss how Jesus fulfills each of the four steps in
the Scripture passages.

Step 1: _____

Read Luke 23:44–46.

Step 2: _____

Read Matthew 26:42.

Step 3: _____

Read Mark 14:32–34.

Step 4: _____

Read John 19:30.

**"The weak channel is clothed with authority
by the Holy Spirit and can speak the word of
deliverance."**

Read John 14:12.

11. Compare and contrast:

a. The grace of faith

_____

_____

b. The gifts of faith

_____

_____

Discussion Question: "The doors of God's treasury had been permanently opened to him, and he could take as much as he needed." What kind of preparation would God have to do in your life before you could handle this type of relationship?

Discussion Question: What are the various areas Blumhardt has to gain before the final victory of access to the Throne?

Personal Question: Can you apply this principle to your circumstances at home or on the job?

Assignment

To keep on keeping on and stay in God's presence when circumstances seem against you, what would you do in the following cases? Choose one of the following: pray, praise, gripe, or thank.

1. Harsh words are spoken _____

2. Complimentary words spoken _____

3. Car gets dent in fender _____

4. Dinner burns _____

5. Money is spent unwisely _____

6. Unexpected company arrives _____

7. You inherit $6,000 _____

Chapter 13: Challenging Death

Discussion Question: What does Rees say about weeping? Why do you have to weep?

Discussion Question: What does God's presence feel like to Rees? What has it felt like to you?

After Rees tells the woman that her dying husband will live, the devil attacks him for several days. It is "a severe test of faith." However, he does not "take note of the Enemy's attacks." As soon as you notice Satan trying to get your attention, or to keep it focused on bad thoughts, don't let him have it or keep it. Get back on a good track. Do not let the devil get your attention!

1. List some of the things you can immediately do to get your mind back from the devil.

_____

_____

_____

_____

_____

_____

The woman's husband is healed, but the next case is more difficult. The vital question is: What is God's will? Only the impartial can find God's will.

"The Lord's will must be revealed in each case."

Read aloud:

> He returned in the early afternoon, because every minute counted. He could even joke with William Davies a bit now, saying, "If I tell you God's will, will you believe me? If you do, and I tell you your wife is to get well, mind there are no more tears! If you want to cry, you had better cry now before I tell you!"

> "The Holy Spirit was in the house," Mr. Howells said, "and I knew He had conquered death. Naturally speaking, death was in the room, but I was in perfect peace. We got down and prayed, about six of the children joining us. What a praise meeting we had, and she changed for the better that day!"

> Through the position gained in his intercession for the tubercular woman, God's servant had become sensitive to His voice in cases of sickness in a way that he had never been before.

> It had been a long spiritual climb in her case, but now he found that in a moment he could take the word of the Lord. He had so many of these cases at that time that it looked as if this would be his special ministry; and he often said from that period that he believed a new era of healing would break forth in the Christian church.

Perhaps only eternity will reveal how much the Spirit's intercession and believing through Him has contributed to the revival of spiritual healing that has been witnessed in many parts of the church in recent years.

2. Complete:

a. "God's servant had become _____

_____ in cases of sickness in a way that he never had before."

b. "But now he found that in a moment he could _____

_____."

Christ delivers believers from the power of death. Read John 3:16; Hebrews 2:14–15.

Assignment

List a few of the many ways God has of getting His will across to you.

_____

_____

_____

_____

_____

Chapter 14: A Father to Orphans

Rees says, "Blood is thicker than water." Yet God replies, "Yes, but *spirit* is thicker than blood!"

We are children of God. Read John 1:12–13; First John 3:1–2; Romans 8:16–17, 19.

Rees tells the Lord, "I am willing for You to be a Father through me, but I cannot do it unless You love them through me, so that they are not like adopted but begotten children. And to do that, You will have to change my nature."

"It was the love of God flowing through me."

Discussion Question: Why is it so important to have the love of God flowing through each one of us?

Read aloud:

> "The place of intercession gained at that time holds good today. There was no need for the Lord to test it over again, unless there had been indifference or backsliding. From that gained position one can continually pray for the orphans and ask the Lord to be a Father to them, even through others, because one only asks Him to do through another what one is willing for the Lord to do through

him or her. This is the law of intercession on every level of life: that only so far as we have been tested and proved willing to do a thing ourselves can we intercede for others. Christ is our Intercessor because He took the place of each one prayed for."

1. Rees says that there will be no need for the Lord to test this position again, unless what two things happen?

a. _____

b. _____

Discussion Question: What is the meaning of each?

Discussion Question: We are not called to intercede for sin—Christ already did that. But, the Lord does call us to intercede for sinners and their needs. "The Holy Spirit can never 'bind the strong man' (Mark 3:27, KJV) through us on a higher level than that in which He has first had victory in us." What does this mean?

Discussion Question: Rees is led to pay the debt on a man's Sick Benefit Club. This happens shortly after the Spirit called Rees to not keep up his own payments to the Club. Rees says, "We cannot say a thing is wrong for others just because we have been called to give it up; it depends on our position or grade in life." What are some of the things you no longer do, that you used to do, and that you now condemn in others?

2. Read and complete the following:

a. Read Romans 14:1, 4, 10, 13.

Complete: We are not to _____ others.

b. Read Matthew 7:1–5.

Complete: We are to judge _____ first.

c. Read Philippians 1:9–11. What would God have us do?

_____

_____

It is hard not to judge others; but when you criticize—especially immature Christians, or those just starting to learn about the love of God—you may hurt their feelings, and even their relationship to Jesus, by not being a loving representative of God. Let people know you disapprove without being hurtful.

"The Holy Spirit was judging by the motive."

Discussion Question: The Lord guides Rees to pay the man's Sick Benefit Club fees. Months later, the love of God breaks the man down. Through this experience, Rees learns that God will keep others through him if he gives perfect obedience to the Holy Spirit. How does obedience to the Holy Spirit allow God to keep others through you?

3. What is the Lord's twofold purpose?

a. _____

b. _____

Personal Question: How is this happening in your life?

Read aloud:

"The Holy Spirit took me through grade after grade. The process of changing one's natures (replacing the self nature by the divine nature) was very slow and bitter. It was a daily dying and showing forth the life of Christ, but that life was the life of a victim. Christ was the greatest Victim on one side of the cross but the greatest Victor on the other. The daily path was the way of the cross; every selfish motive and every selfish thought was at once dealt with by the Holy Spirit. The strictest man I knew in my boyhood days was my schoolmaster, but how often I said that the Holy Spirit was a thousand times more strict—the schoolmaster could only judge by actions, but the Holy Spirit was judging by the motive."

4. Rees' life in Christ "was a life of fullest liberty." Is your life full of liberty or bondages? List liberties or bondages here.

_____

_____

_____

_____

_____

The devil is the captor. Read Second Timothy 2:26.

Christ releases us from all bondages. Read John 8:34–36; Galatians 5:1; Romans 8:21.

5. Why does the devil want captives?

_____

_____

_____

Prayer: *We ask that the Holy Spirit bring to mind those things that keep us in bondage, and that by the power in the Name of Jesus these things be removed.*

Consider this a deliverance, not a loss.

Assignment

Read Isaiah 61:1–3 and list all the things the Spirit of the Lord is going to do through you.

_____

_____

_____

_____

_____

_____

_____

_____

_____

What will you be called?

_____

What will you display?

_____

Chapter 15: Lord Radstock

1. Complete:

a. "_____ can pray for things to be done, without necessarily being willing for the answers to come through themselves; and they are not even bound to continue in the prayers until they are answered."

b. "But _____ are responsible to gain their objectives, and they can never be free until they have gained them."

Discussion Question: Discuss the differences between prayer warriors and intercessors.

Read aloud:

> During his address Mr. Howells also touched on divine healing, and told of the Lord's dealings with him over the tubercular woman: how the first gained case had to go to the altar, because the firstfruits belong to God; and how, although the Holy Spirit witnessed in him that he had gained it, he had to walk it as a failure; and how, through that, the Lord gave such a sentence of death to the flesh that in all future cases of healing self would take no glory.

Pride can so easily come. You have to be aware of it and know that it is only because you have the presence of God that you have His power, and that *all the glory belongs to God!*

"Self would take no glory."

2. Look up the word *pride*.

_____

_____

3. Read Mark 7:20–23 (KJV). Where does pride come from?

_____

4. Read Psalm 73:6–8. Referring to the prosperous wicked, what is their necklace?

_____

5. Read Proverbs 13:10 (KJV); 16:18. What are the results of pride?

_____

_____

_____

Personal Question: When there is a quarrel at home, what is usually at the root of it, in you?

6. Read Romans 12:3. What are God's instructions to us?

_____

_____

_____

_____

7. Read Proverbs 16:5 (KJV). What is God's opinion of the prideful?

_____

8. Read Isaiah 25:11–12. What will be God's judgment on the proud?

_____

_____

_____

Beware of pride—especially when walking in the gifts of the Spirit.

Assignment

Put an "x" next to the statements that we like to think show humility but are really prideful.

( ) I'm not worthy.

( ) They don't want me to go.

( ) I'm uncomfortable in their presence.

( ) I don't know how, and am sure I can't learn.

( ) I'll stay home rather than walk with a cane.

( ) Nobody gives to me; why should I give to them?

( ) Open their eyes to your Word, Lord, so they can be good like me!

( ) God only uses people walking in the Spirit like me.

Add two of your own.

1. _____

2. _____

Chapter 16: Called to a Hidden Life

Discussion Question: Some men in the village—though they attend the meetings and have a desire to follow Christ—continue to be "terrible slaves to drink." What does this tell you about most bad habits?

"The Enemy still kept his hold on them."

1. Read Matthew 12:29; 16:19. Write a prayer that addresses these words of God about setting the captives free.

_____

_____

_____

_____

_____

Discussion Question: "Oh, how precious the name of Jesus was to us!" What does the name of Jesus mean to you? Read Acts 3:6, 16.

2. While walking to the mission, Rees takes off his hat and "continue[s] in the attitude of prayer." What does that phrase mean to you?

_____

_____

_____

_____

_____

Discussion Question: What does his cap come to signify for Rees?

Keep in the attitude of prayer all day.

Read aloud:

> "How much of the world is in us, when we often think we are dead to it!" commented Mr. Howells. "I used to laugh about a man who had put the Salvation Army cap on, but I wished that day that the Holy Spirit would allow me to wear even that! But He would allow no compromise. I had to say, 'I am a bondslave; You pull me through.'"

Discussion Question: How does the world influence you and keep you from walking in the holiness of God?

Personal Question: Do you compromise on things you know the Lord has instructed you to do His way, by continuing to doing them your way?

The Lord will deal with us about seemingly simple things in our lives, but they could be big blocks in keeping Him from flowing in us the way He wants to.

Read aloud:

> "I shall never forget going through the town that day and passing people going to other churches. Talk about being dead to the world! Every sensitive nerve in me was alive to the world's influence! I was not much better than a blind person. It seemed that the devil had gathered all the forces of hell to attack this simple obedience. In itself, there was nothing to it; I was only called to spend the day in the attitude of prayer and that meant a little separation from the world.

> "Oh, the depths of this respectable self-nature—but it was in the process of being changed for the divine nature! It was a deliverance to reach the mission. It was like the city of refuge from the avenger of blood, and among ourselves there was always a laugh after a test."

3. Complete:

"It seemed that the _____ had gathered all the forces of hell to attack this _____ _____."

If the devil goes that all-out to keep us from obeying the Word of God, then obedience to the Word must be a powerful weapon that will wipe him out!

4. List some of the ways you can wipe Satan out of your life, and keep him out.

_____

_____

_____

_____

_____

"In separating him to Himself, the Lord was preparing to take Rees much farther than this. He was going to call him away from public ministry altogether and the next step came through an attack of the Enemy on his special friend and coworker in the mission." Read Second Corinthians 6:17–18.

Discussion Question: The Enemy's attack on Rees' friend is serious, and the Lord shows Rees that only he can help his friend. He has to step down as leader of the mission and instead be an intercessor for his friend. How, in certain instances, are you the only one who can help save or influence a person that God is trying to get into His Kingdom?

Read aloud:

> "For three years I had put all my time, money and everything into the mission and had been over every night. And now, when there were great prospects, He was asking me to step down and help behind my friend, as he had previously helped behind me. The mission was growing, and would become still more popular, and the people naturally would attribute all the success to my friend. They would never see nor remember that it needed someone to put down the foundation.
>
> "It was a great inward conflict to allow my friend to get the outward success. This was the next grade of self the Holy Spirit was going to deal with; and it was a hard process, allowing self to be replaced by His divine nature. For three

days I could not willingly accept it, but I knew I would be pulled through. It was God's way of working one up to having as much joy in a hidden life as in an open and successful one. If my aim in life was to do God's will, then I could truly say either way would be equal joy."

Personal Question: Is your aim in life to do God's will or your will? Read Matthew 12:50; First John 5:14–15.

"God brought Rees through and made another deep change in his nature." Remember, it is God who replaces self with His nature.

Assignment

Look back over the past ten years and list some of the changes God has made in you.

_____

_____

_____

_____

_____

So, remember to be patient with your loved ones; it took a while for you to come around also.

Assignment for during the week: Keep in an attitude of prayer all day, and write the results here.

_____

_____

_____

Chapter 17: The Hatless Brigade

Rees receives a letter from Mr. Gosset, asking him to visit him in London. Rees decides that he cannot make this trip, because he was just called to gain a new place of intercession. However, the Lord knows that this is not the true reason. The text says, "The Holy Spirit would always probe down to the very root of the self He wanted to get at." Rees confesses that he doesn't want to go to London and be Mr. Gosset's guest without his hat.

Personal Question: "The hundred and one excuses the flesh made! But the Holy Spirit would have none of them." Do you make excuses to God?

Read aloud:

> The conflict was sharp. It even came into his mind momentarily whether it was possible to turn back from this life of surrender, this bondslave life, this daily dying—just live an ordinary Christian life, preach the gospel and help the poor as many of his friends did.

> But the Spirit held him to the reality of his "living martyr" position, with no more claim on his life down here than a dead person has.

There was some questioning, as there always was until he actually came up to becoming one with the Holy Spirit in what He was doing, but he knew he had no choice in the matter, and he would not dare show any real unwillingness lest he should forfeit the privilege of his martyr position.

Discussion Question: What does it mean to become one with the Holy Spirit? Read First Corinthians 6:17; 12:12–13.

"Yes, Lord; You pull me through!"

"The Spirit 'who never pushes' drew him with the cords of love." Draw in your loved ones with the cords of love.

Assignment

List the cords of love you use.

_____

_____

_____

_____

_____

Chapter 18: The Vow of a Nazarite

Discussion Question: "The Holy Spirit would be his Teacher."
How would this apply in all the things you do?

1. What does it mean to wait before the Lord?

_____

_____

_____

Discussion Question: "To silence the voices of self . . . [provides] access into the presence of God." What are the voices of self?

Read Psalm 16:11; First Chronicles 17:27 (KJV).

Read aloud:

> "I saw how the iniquity of the nation was laid upon Ezekiel,
> but I wasn't afraid of being tested in food like him (see
> Ezek. 4). Neither was I afraid of Jeremiah, but I *was* afraid
> of Isaiah! There was never a prophet like that man—of royal
> blood and one of the greatest statesmen and writers. But I
> saw how the Holy Spirit humiliated him in what He called
> him to do (see Isa. 20). The only comfort I had was that

by starting to read at Genesis, it would take me about two months before I reached him! But much sooner than that I reached something else and I couldn't escape it."

Read Isaiah 20. Consider how specifically God speaks to Isaiah. The Holy Spirit will give you specific instructions.

Read aloud Rees' conversation with the Holy Spirit about why he does not want to "walk like Samuel and John the Baptist."

> **"He knew he had to go through with it. As usual, Rees had to say, 'Pull me through!' and, indeed, he needed pulling."**

Rees' family quickly figures out that something is wrong—he doesn't go out at night, he stays back from chapel, and he doesn't shave. It is painful, but he cannot give his family an explanation, for the path is: "He opened not his mouth" (Isa. 53:7). Read Mark 15:5; Isaiah 53:7.

2. Read and discuss Rees' observation and revelation about Will Battery. What is the only reason Rees does all of these things?

_____

_____

_____

3. "But if at the beginning the world was affecting him, by the end it was he who was affecting the world, for people sensed the presence of God with him, and said so." What are some of the reactions to Rees during this time?

_____

_____

_____

Read aloud:

> "In two weeks I had the victory and became dead to the
> influence of the world. It was as Paul said, 'This light
> momentary affliction is preparing for us an eternal weight
> of glory beyond all comparison' (2 Cor. 4:17). Oh the glory
> of that inward life! The three hours in the evening were
> a time spent in glory; it was nothing less than the Word
> being illuminated by the Holy Spirit. What perfect peace
> the Spirit gave me and what love for a lost soul!"

Read Second Corinthians 4:17–18.

**"It was the process of sanctification, when the
self-nature and all its lusts had to be exchanged
for the divine nature."**

4. Read Romans 6:6–7; Second Peter 1:4. Can you see daily
progress along these lines?

_____

_____

_____

Discussion Question: What is meant by "wonderful liberty in
the presence of God"?

Assignment

Write out two verses that show that a soul is a very precious commodity.

1. _____

_____

_____

_____

_____

2. _____

_____

_____

_____

_____

Chapter 19: Uncle Dick's Healing

Read aloud:

> [Rees] chose to continue the hidden life because, he said, "The fellowship I had had with the Lord Himself surpassed all I ever had with man, also I had not finished going through the Bible with the Holy Spirit. The hardest thing in my life had become the sweetest."

1. List some of the things that were hardest in your life, but have now become the sweetest.

_____

_____

_____

_____

_____

The Lord reminds Rees that before you can intercede for someone, you must live like him or her. Since the child widows of India were living on one handful of rice a day, Rees chooses to eat one meal of porridge every two days. This is not easy for Rees. However, he says, "When you take the place of another, you take the suffering of another; you have to walk every inch of it." He fasts like this for ten weeks, saying, "Each fast, if carried out under the guidance of the Holy Spirit, means that our bodies become more equipped to carry burdens."

> **The point of fasting is to bring the body into subjection to the Spirit.**

There are no set rules in the Bible for fasting. A fast can be short or long. You can give up one item or a whole meal. It must always be done under the leading and guidance of the Holy Spirit: the reason, the time, and what is to be given up.

Discussion Question: What experiences have you had with fasting?

2. Read Ezra 8:21, 23. Circle items that pertain to these verses.

Proclaimed   in humbleness   in pride   as a group
as an individual   asking for a safe journey   fasted and prayed
cried in disbelief   God answered

3. Read Jonah 3:5, 8–9. Rewrite this in modern-day language, pertaining to you.

_____

_____

_____

_____

_____

4. Read Jonah 3:10. What are the results of fasting and repentance in Nineveh?

_____

_____

_____

Personal Question: Would God also do this for your family and nation?

5. Look up the word *sackcloth*.

_____

_____

6. Read Matthew 17:14–21 (KJV); Mark 9:14–29 (KJV). What happens through prayer and fasting in these passages?

_____

_____

_____

Discussion Question: What circumstances in your life might need this kind of prayer, accompanied by fasting?

Prayer and fasting is the master key to the impossible.

Rees' Uncle Dick is an invalid and cannot walk. One morning the Holy Spirit speaks to him and tells him that it is the Lord's will to restore Uncle Dick. When Rees arrives at Pentwyn, he tells his uncle this news. His uncle's initial response is to go away and pray to the Lord about it.

When he returns he says to Rees that he will be healed, and he gives Rees the exact date. By committing to a date, Grubb says, "It was to be as much of a reality to them then as it would be to other people after it became a fact."

Read aloud:

> "This was not a case of the fight of faith," said Mr. Howells, "but of standing still and seeing the salvation of the Lord."

Faith is the realization of things hoped for, the proof of things not seen.

7. Copy Hebrews 11:1 from the Living Bible here.

_____

_____

_____

_____

_____

8. Complete:

"The Holy Spirit warned them _____

_____. If they did, their prayers would be _____

_____."

Read aloud:

> It was the last attack of the Enemy, who whispered, "It is all up. You are just the same now as any other night, and you have only got three hours." One minute is quite long

enough for the Lord. He went back to bed, and deep sleep came over him.

The next thing the uncle heard was the clock striking five, and he found himself perfectly restored. He called the family up, and there was such a solemn awe in the house that they were afraid to move, realizing that God Himself had done that great act that very hour.

Discussion Question: Relate the sovereignty of God to this situation and similar ones in your life.

Read aloud:

> Mr. Howells' comment was, "If I had doubted, would I have rejoiced? The Lord will never give the witness unless we believe; and if we believe, we can afford the delay. To me there was something greater than the healing—it was the further confirmation that the position of intercession had been gained, and could be used in any case where God willed it."

Assignment

Explain what part intercession has to do with the healing of Rees' uncle.

_____

_____

_____

_____

_____

Chapter 20: Called Out from Wage-Earning

Read aloud:

> It is hard to realize that throughout these three years of intense conflict and many triumphs in the Spirit, Rees Howells was working daily at one of the hardest jobs a man can do—down the mine, cutting coal. His was no sheltered, monastic life, but a walk in the Spirit right in the world, though never of it.

1. What do you think is the most dynamic part of this paragraph?

_____

_____

_____

Read Genesis 1:26.

We are made in the image of the God who created this universe. He has given us the ability to know Him, to be filled with His Spirit, to be like Him, and to walk in His Holy Spirit. And when you walk in the Spirit, you walk in love.

Some older versions of the Bible use the word *charity* rather than "love." And according to *Unger's Bible Dictionary*, the only Bible word translated "charity" really means "love." *Its absence invalidates all claims to the Christian name.*

2. Read Second Corinthians 13:4–5. With this passage in mind, write your definition of what love is.

_____

_____

_____

_____

Personal Question: Is that description a picture of you?

3. When you walk in the Spirit, you *listen* to the voice of God. When you walk in the Spirit, you *obey* the voice of God. What results are we promised if we listen to and obey God? Read Proverbs 8:32–35.

_____

_____

_____

Discussion Question: What does it mean to receive God's favor?

4. When you walk in the Spirit you trust and abide in the Lord. Does this mean you rely on God once in a while, or all the time? Read Proverbs 3:5–6; Psalm 91:1–2.

_____

_____

_____

Read aloud:

> Rees was standing on a small wooden bridge across a little stream, and the Lord asked him, "Will you give your word to Me that you won't look to another person to keep you? If so, put up your hand and repeat, 'I shall not take from a thread to a shoe latchet from any person, unless the Lord tells me.'"

> Just as Abraham made that stand when he refused the spoils of war that were justly his, lest men should say his prosperity came from natural sources (see Gen. 14:22–23), so God was asking His servant to take this same stand for the rest of his life. On that bridge he raised his hand and made the solemn vow, adding, "I do believe You are able to keep me better than that mining company."

"The Lord was impressing on him that the real life of faith meant receiving all that he needed from God."

5. After Rees' mother agrees to let Rees pay her for his lodgings, the Lord allows Rees to have a month's holiday. What does Rees Howells do on this vacation?

_____

_____

_____

Personal Question: The devil bothers Rees with negative thoughts. The Lord tells him, "Don't allow the devil to speak to you again." Can you do that? Work at it.

On the day before his rent is due, Rees' father gives him a bad time; and while they are speaking, the postman arrives with a letter for Rees. It is from Mr. Gossett, offering him a position in the London City Mission, at a salary of 100 pounds a year. "It was a good beginning to forty years of praying and abundantly proving the Lord's Prayer, 'Give us this day our daily bread' (Matt. 6:11)."

Assignment

Read and reflect on the Lord's Prayer. Rewrite it as a personal letter from you to God.

> Pray then like this:
> "Our Father in heaven,
> hallowed be your name.
> Your kingdom come,
> your will be done,
>   on earth as it is in heaven.
> Give us this day our daily bread,
> and forgive us our debts,
>   as we also have forgiven our debtors.
> And lead us not into temptation,
>   but deliver us from evil."
>   (Matt. 6:9–13)

_____

_____

Chapter 21: Madeira

Joe Evans has a hemorrhage in his lungs, and he goes to Rees for guidance. Rees tells Joe to follow the doctor's advice. This may seem like he isn't trusting in the Lord. However, "God had taught him that He steps in when natural remedies have failed." He says to Joe, "Probably the Lord wants to show that medicine can't do it."

While reflecting on this time, Rees says, "If the Holy Spirit had not taught me that I was only to pray the prayers He gives, I would have taken up my friend's case long before that. It was a proof that, though the place of intercession was gained, I could only use it as led by the Spirit."

Discussion Question: What does Rees mean when he says he can only use the gained place of intercession as led by the Spirit?

Joe's stay at the sanatorium does not appear to help. The doctor suggests that he go to a tropical climate to avoid the cold winter. Joe's family cannot afford it; but that same day, Rees receives a gift—and he offers it to Joe's father. Rees says of Joe's father, "He saw God's love making him equal to a rich man. I thought it was worth it all if only to reach him."

The Lord then tells Rees to go with Joe to Madeira. Elizabeth prays about this and the Lord asks her, "If Rees had been the tubercular and another person had offered to go with him, would she not have accepted that? And does not the Word say, 'Whatever you wish that others would do to you, do also to them' (Matt. 7:12)?"

Personal Question: Can you truly say this is how you treat others: "Do to others as you would have them do to you"?

Know that when God is leading, He always has a special purpose in all He has you do or in what He provides.

Discussion Question: Rees begins to feel resentment towards the missionary. He says, "I took care of my mind; but this began to be magnified in me and I found something in me which prevented me from loving him." What does he mean by, "I took care of my mind"?

"I brought you to Madeira, to this place, to show you the difference between My love and yours; and to show you that there is something in your nature that I need to rid you of." Love others who do something against you.

Read aloud:

> "I praised God for finding this out in me. I was to love the missionary, not for what he gave me but because I couldn't help loving him. I could see the root of the Savior's nature was love, and if the root of mine was love, nothing the missionary did could affect me. I saw it in a flash, and went on my knees, and asked the Holy Spirit not to move me from that place till I came through. Supposing I had

remained blind and a fool, and gone on preaching the Sermon on the Mount with this in my nature! If ever I loved the Savior, it was then. I saw Him loving those who put Him to death—and there are no limits to that love."

Personal Question: Would you like to function like that?

Discussion Question: What kind of results would it produce in your family if you functioned like that?

> **"I could see the root of the Savior's nature was love, and if the root of mine was love, nothing the missionary did could affect me."**

1. "I lost sight of my friend, and lived with the Savior who is perfect, holy. I saw what it would be when I gained the position." What are the three items Rees will receive?

a. _____

b. _____

c. _____

2. Complete:

"But in six weeks _____,
as much as a drunkard is changed when he sees what the Savior has done for him. I changed _____."

Personal Question: Can you see how God is working in your life to bring you into that perfect love?

3. Look up the word *love*.

_____

_____

4. Read Matthew 22:37–40. What is the greatest command-
   ment? What is the second?

a. _____

b. _____

5. Read First John 4:16.

a. What is God?

_____

b. If you are His child, what should you be?

_____

6. Read Romans 5:5. Where does this love come from?

_____

7. Read Ephesians 3:17–20. In order to be filled with all the
   fullness of God, what must you be rooted and grounded in?

_____

Discussion Question: How will God's love overcome the world?

Regarding his friend Joe: "This sickness is not unto death, but
for the glory of God."

Regarding hearing the voice of God: "As I entered the little train . . . I heard that Voice which I know as really as a child knows his father's voice. It said, 'By a month today Joe will be restored.' The glory of God came down on the train."

Discussion Question: How has the voice of God become more distinct in your life since starting this study?

> **"'When everything of nature and medicine had failed,' the Lord showed him that 'a higher law was going to operate.'"**

8. Complete:

"It has never happened before because of_____."

Rees explains, "God doesn't step in with a spiritual law till the end of the law of nature has been reached." There is nothing more that medicine can do, and it appears to Joe and Rees that "the law of nature was at an end." This case doesn't require prayer. The Lord says He would heal Joe, and they trust His word.

The Holy Spirit asks Rees if he will send the cable, before Joe has been healed. Read aloud Rees' telling of this story.

9. Complete:

"If you take the healing from Me against _____
_____and _____
_____, you will have gained a
_____than in your uncle's healing."

Discuss this statement.

10. Complete:

"Only a _____ in

_____ could make me do it."

11. List some of the things you can do to strengthen yourself
to believe God's Word against what you see.

_____

_____

_____

_____

_____

Discussion Question: What does "the victory of faith" mean?

Sometimes after your greatest victories comes a time of testing.

12. Read Hebrews 11:1. What is faith?

_____

13. Read Romans 1:17. How do the righteous live?

_____

Discussion Question: Can you see by the evidence of people's
lives whether they are living by faith or not? How?

14. Read Luke 8:10. What are you given as the result of faith?

_____

Discussion Question: How valuable is this knowledge?

Assignment

List three more verses on the results of faith.

1._____

_____

_____

2._____

_____

_____

3._____

_____

_____

Chapter 22:
Marriage and Missionary Call

Read aloud the first paragraphs of this chapter, which tell of the events that happen before Rees and Elizabeth's wedding.

1. What is the most dynamic part of that story?

_____

_____

_____

2. Complete:

a. "What a privilege it was to . . . proclaim the _____

_____ of _____!"

b. "There is no glory like that of proclaiming the _____."

c. "I was called to preach more about _____."

3. What the results will be in a person's life when he or she believes in eternal life through Christ?

_____

_____

_____

"Then, in the midst of all this, God called again." Rees and Elizabeth begin to pray after Rees receives a vision of Africa from the Lord. At first, they think the purpose of the vision was to burden them to pray for someone else to go. But the Lord reveals to them that *they* should be the ones to go. Rees says, "With the Lord we can only push others as far as we are willing to be pushed ourselves. There were a thousand and one hindrances, but the Lord would take no excuses—where there's a will, there's a way!"

4. Look up the word *excuse*.

_____

_____

5. Read Luke 14:16–21. What does the Master do after all these excuses?

_____

_____

Personal Question: What do you think is God's attitude toward some of your excuses to Him?

When you take your hands off, the Lord can move in perfection.

Read aloud the story of Rees and Elizabeth's first test, to give up their son and devote their time to their work.

Discussion Question: What does Rees mean by "we wouldn't have dared to interfere"?

"We were coming up to the victory by degrees; the process was slow and hard. Because it was going to be an intercession, one had to walk every inch."

6. Read Philippians 4:13. Who is your strength?

_____

_____

"Giving our best to the Lord."

When you give something up, you are sacrificing. Sacrifice is giving up something of value to obtain something of greater value! Read Ephesians 5:2.

Assignment

List things you have given up as sacrifices. Then list what you have received of a much greater value.

Sacrifice: Received:

Sacrifice: Received:

Sacrifice: Received:

Chapter 23: Standing in the Queue

1. Mr. Albert Head says to Rees, "The Lord has been speaking to me through you. I have never 'kept' a missionary before, but God has told me to keep you as my missionary. No one else is to support you, and while you are preaching in Africa, I will share in the harvest!" How can you share in a harvest?

_____

_____

_____

2. Complete:

"There is nothing in the world better for strengthening one's faith than _____!"

Personal Question: While Mrs. Howells is training in Scotland and Rees is in London for a nine-month medical course, they experience "trials of faith, and deliverances." Of this time Rees says, "We were in the school of faith . . . and there is nothing to be compared with having to be delivered to keep you abiding; you will never do it without." What is your school of faith?

Read First Peter 5:7.

3. Read Isaiah 58:11–12. What two names will the one who does this be called?

a. _____

b. _____

Discussion Question: Rees says, "When we have a very hard thing to do, He will burden us in another way to make the former one easier!" Discuss this statement and what it meant in Rees and Elizabeth's situation. Have you had any similar experiences?

> "In cases of giving medicine, it depends wholly on guidance; if the Holy Spirit leads a person not to give it, He will be sure to make up for it."

Discussion Question: "Our extremity would be God's opportunity." What does this mean?

Read aloud:

"The Spirit then spoke to me and said, 'If you had money, what would you do?'

"'Take my place in the queue at the booking office,' I said.

"'Well, are you not preaching that My promises are equal to current coin? You had better take your place in the queue.'

"So there was nothing I could do except obey.

"There were about a dozen people before me. There they were passing by the booking office one by one. The devil kept telling me, 'Now you have only a few people in front of you, and when your turn comes, you will have to walk through. You have preached much about Moses with the Red Sea in front and the Egyptians behind (see Exod. 14), but now you are the one who is shut in.'

"'Yes, shut in,' I answered, 'but like Moses, I'll be gloriously led out'

"When there were only two before me, a man stepped out of the crowd and said, 'I'm sorry I can't wait any longer, but I must open my shop.' He said good-bye and put thirty shillings in my hand! It was most glorious, and only a foretaste of what the Lord would do in Africa, if we would obey. After I had the tickets, the people who came with us to the train began to give gifts to us, but the Lord had held them back until we had been tested. We were singing all the way to London!"

Discussion Question: How does the hand of God move in Rees' experience in the queue?

4. Complete:

"It was most _____, and only a _____ of what the Lord would do in Africa, if we would _____."

5. Read Exodus 19:5–6. If you like Israel are obedient, what will you be to God?

_____

6. Read First Samuel 15:22. What does God desire rather than sacrifice?

_____

7. Read Isaiah 1:18–20. If you are willing and obedient, what happens? If you refuse and rebel, what will happen?

_____

_____

8. Read Romans 5:19. Who is that "one man"?

_____

9. Read Hebrews 5:8–9.

Complete: Jesus "learned _____ through what He suffered. . . . He became the source of eternal salvation to all who _____ Him."

Discussion Question: Do these verses teach salvation by works?

Read aloud:

> They had all their outfit except three things: a watch, a fountain pen and a raincoat each. They had never mentioned these things to anyone, but at breakfast Mr. Head asked, "What kind of watches have you?" and told them that his son, Alfred, wanted to give them a watch each.
>
> He then asked, "Have you prepared for the rainy seasons in Africa? Have you got good raincoats?"

When they said they hadn't, he told them to go and get one each; and he wrote down an address on a card, saying that they were to get them at his expense.

After writing the address, he asked, "Have you seen this kind of fountain pen?" They said no. "You must take one each with you," he said. The three things they had named to the Lord, he named to them!

Discussion Question: Have you ever had a similar experience?

"Knowing that the One who had called them into this life was able to deliver in all circumstances."

Assignment

Write a dynamic prayer, asking the Father to help you obtain a faith like Rees Howells had when he stood in that queue.

_____

_____

_____

_____

_____

Chapter 24: Revivals in Africa

Founded in 1889, the South Africa General Mission's purpose was to spread the gospel throughout the unevangelized parts of South Africa. The Howells join this mission and are sent to Rusitu Mission Station in Gazaland, near the border of what is now Mozambique. The people there know that the Howells came from a land that had just experienced a revival, and they ask if they brought revival with them. Rees tells them that "the source of all revival is the Holy Spirit," and that the Holy Spirit can do among them what He did in Wales. Rees continues to preach about revival; and soon after the Howells' arrival, the Spirit starts to move among the believers.

1. Look up the word *revive*.

_____

_____

2. Read Isaiah 57:15; Hosea 6:2–3. What is the reason God is reviving and restoring us?

_____

_____

_____

Discussion Question: What does your conclusion about revival and restoration mean to you?

Read aloud Rees' account of the days that followed the Holy Spirit's arrival.

"Truly 'sowing in tears' the seed of life with patience and prayer. . . . The Spirit doing a mighty convicting work in souls and leading to confessions such as no human agency could have extorted from them."

3. Complete:

"The men who had held back somewhat in the morning coming forward in _____,
and completely _____;
. . . and this went on without any _____ under
the _____."

4. What are some of the "little flames that are already alight" in Rees' story?

_____

_____

_____

5. By what can we fan the flames of revival into a mighty blaze?

_____

_____

_____

"'I was pleading on His word, Malachi 3:10, and I *saw* the Holy Spirit descending. He appeared to me, I *saw* Him coming down on all the mission stations,' and the glory of God was so much on him that he was not in himself." Read Malachi 3:10.

> **"The Holy Spirit was going in us, and He is the Author of Pentecost and the Source of revival."**

6. Complete:

"If you have sinned against God, it is between

_____ and _____; but

if you have sinned against _____, you must

confess before _____."

Discussion Question: What can a dynamic testimony do? Why?

Discussion Question: "On the third day, the power that was there! It wasn't the preaching; it was the power!" How is the Holy Spirit your power source?

Read aloud:

> In ways like these the Holy Spirit came down on every station and gave revival—exactly as He had said He would do—and fulfilled the promise of the ten thousand souls.

> In Johannesburg, for instance, Mr. Howells conducted great revival meetings for twenty-one days in one of the largest churches and it was packed every night. He had to speak through three interpreters, there were so many different tribes, but that did not hinder the Spirit

breaking through and hundreds coming out every night for salvation.

No one was more conscious than His servant that the Holy Spirit was the doer of it, and that it was "not by might, nor by power, but by my Spirit" (Zech. 4:6).

He laid hands on hundreds under the Spirit's power and guidance, and they came free every time. Outside the meetings he would look at his hands, see how ordinary they were and wonder where the power came from! But he knew!

Read Zechariah 4:6.

The great influenza epidemic begins to reach Rees' district, and many are affected by it. Rees is discouraged by this, as the "break" among many of the married men has just begun. The Lord responds to Rees' trouble with Romans 8:28, and He says to him, "Can't you trust Me that this is a blessing in disguise?"

7. Write out Romans 8:28. Get this verse into your spirit, and when things go wrong, repeat it to yourself!

_____

_____

_____

_____

_____

"The Holy Spirit said to him, 'Why don't you ask the Father to heal you?' He thought he had, but the Spirit said to him, 'You didn't ask believing.'"

In response to the flu reaching the station, Rees says, "The witch doctors have failed and the ancestral spirits have failed—but our God has not failed."

8. Read Deuteronomy 31:8. Write this verse out in your own words, pertaining to you.

_____

_____

_____

_____

_____

"The Holy Spirit was stronger than death."

Discussion Question: Rees is able to promise that no one will die at the mission station because he knows the Holy Spirit is stronger than death. How can knowing this help you in future times of tribulation?

9. Rees praises God for his "personal Guide!" Who is this personal Guide?

_____

10. Is He available to you?

_____

11. List some of the things He has recently guided you into or through.

_____

_____

_____

_____

_____

At one point, Rees starts to think that he might be getting the disease. However, the Lord says to him, "Don't you believe that I can keep the germ from overcoming you?"

Discussion Question: How are your body and mind protected by the indwelling Holy Spirit? Read Psalm 91:1–7.

Read aloud:

> "I found the Holy Spirit in me was stronger than the flu. What it was to live with God in a plague!

> "I had two cases which tested me very much. If the devil could take them, he could take about fifty. I did everything medically for them, but I couldn't move the temperature, no matter what I tried. So I brought them before the Lord, and pleaded His Word. The moment I got victory, their temperatures dropped and they were safe. There was not a single death."

> The news spread that the God of the white man was stronger than death.

In order to receive the promises of God, they had to work in faith and obedience—and do exactly as God told them.

Read Second Timothy 1:1.

12. Of their time in Africa, Rees says, "I don't think we had anything to cause us an hour's trouble, and for both my wife and myself, they were the six happiest years of our lives." How could anyone say they weren't caused any trouble with all the sickness going on around them?

_____

_____

_____

Assignment

Meditation, and the Power of the Spirit
"This Book of the Law shall not depart from your mouth, but you shall meditate on it day and night, so that you may be careful to do according to all that is written in it. For then you will make your way prosperous, and then you will have good success" (Josh. 1:8).

Results of Meditation
"Call to me and I will answer you, and will tell you great and hidden things that you have not known" (Jer. 33:3).

Instructions:
1. Sit quietly before the Lord your God. Know that He is God, your heavenly Father. Worship and adore Him. Read this verse from Zechariah: "Then he said to me, 'This is the word of the LORD to Zerubbabel: Not by might, nor by power, but by my Spirit, says the LORD of hosts'" (4:6).
2. Meditate on the above verses.
3. Ask the Lord to tell you great and unsearchable things you do not know, to show you on the "television screen of your mind" what He wants you to know.

4. Write on the lines what He has revealed to you.

_____

_____

_____

_____

_____

_____

_____

_____

_____

_____

Chapter 25:
Buying the First Estate in Wales

1. The Lord tells Rees that He is going to build a college through him. This declaration shocks Rees, and he asks the Lord to confirm it through the Word. Summarize the three scriptural promises that stand out to Rees.

a._____

_____

b._____

_____

c._____

_____

Discussion Question: "[The college] meant new and large financial burdens, for the Lord told them that they would have to do it by faith, whereas in their present word all finances were provided." Has the Lord ever told you to do something by faith?

2. Complete:

They "gave themselves over to _____

to be _____ to raise
up a college. . . . They would not have left the mission and the
coworkers they had learned to love for anything less than a direct
_____."

Personal Question: Are you an instrument of God?

"They had no idea where the College was to be. Like Abraham
(see Gen. 12:1), they went out not knowing where they went.
. . . The moment we went to Mumbles [a seaside village near
the city of Swansea], I knew it was the place where God wanted
us to be."

3. Rees asks the Lord to show him if the college should be in
   Swansea. What does God say to him?

   _____

   _____

4. What does God say when Rees and Elizabeth see the vacant
   estate?

   _____

   _____

Personal Question: Can you hear God's voice like that?

5. Read Hebrews 1:1–2 (TLB). How does God speak to us
   today?

   _____

6. Read Revelation 3:20. What happens when we listen?

_____

7. Read John 8:47. Who cannot hear God?

_____

8. What will happen to Rees if the proof does not come?

a. _____

b. _____

9. What will happen to Rees if the proof does come?

a. _____

b. _____

Personal Question: Read Psalm 37:5–6; First Timothy 6:12. Can you apply these two passages to your life right now?

10. How does the devil try to discourage Rees from talking to Mr. Edwards?

_____

_____

_____

Read aloud Rees' explanation of what happens after Mr. Edwards offers Glynderwen to him for £6,300.

11. "I came to the place where I knew that whenever God wants to take over a property, the owner has very little to do with it!" Write about how this principle could apply to your everyday life.

_____

_____

_____

_____

_____

12. Rees receives a letter from Mr. Edwards saying that he is going to sell the estate to someone else. What was Rees' response to this?

_____

_____

_____

_____

_____

Discussion Question: Why are we sometimes affected by the things other people do? What should our response be?

Once you have heard His voice, know He is in charge!

Discussion Question: Discuss the moments of God's perfect abilities and timing in Rees' purchasing of the estate. Have you had any similar moments in your life?

Read aloud:

> But the real battle came over the full sum to be paid. He had never dealt in large amounts before, and the burden was great upon him. He was to take no meetings, nor make any appeals. His eyes were to be on God alone.

> He gave himself to prayer, spending his days in his little upstairs bedroom in his mother's home, alone with God and His Word from six o'clock in the morning to five in the evening, when he took his first meal. In the evenings he continued in prayer with his newly found prayer-partner, Mr. Tommy Howells. Ten months were spent in this way until the victory was complete.

"His eyes were to be on God alone."

Read Second Chronicles 20:12.

Personal Question: God promises him the money, but Rees has to pray it in. Can you visualize the miraculous results in your life if you could touch on this kind of communion with God?

God is our Provider. Read Haggai 2:8, and discuss how it relates to this chapter.

13. Read Psalm 37:3–7.

a. What are you told to do?

_____

b. If you delight yourself in the Lord, what will He give you?

_____

c. What will He do if you commit your way to Him?

_____

d. Complete: "Be still before the LORD and _____

_____ for him."

14. In what way does the Lord lead Rees differently than Müller?

_____

_____

_____

_____

_____

Discussion Question: What allows God to work on behalf of getting Rees the money he needed?

The moment he believed, God moved.

Discussion Question: Rees has the option to take the easy way out and accept an offer to buy the tavern, thus supplying the extra money they needed. It is a "serious temptation" for Rees to take the "easy way of deliverance." Can you give some examples of this in your own life?

Assignment

List six things in your life that would not have happened without prayer.

1. _____

2. _____

3. _____

4. _____

5. _____

6. _____

Chapter 26:
The Bible College of Wales

1. "But no work of God can become established unless it goes through the fire." Look up the word *fire* in a Bible dictionary.

_____

_____

Read Matthew 3:11.

"The Lord warned him that trouble was coming, but that through it He would purge the work, to His own glory."

Read Malachi 3:2–3.

Discussion Question: What has been the process of your refinement?

Read aloud:

> For twelve months they didn't have a single lecture, and many thought the college would never rise again. But the time was spent shut in with God in prayer, and they were

able to prove that the work did not depend on human support or popularity.

"Through this experience," said Mr. Howells, "the college was put on the Rock of Ages, on a foundation that no man nor devil could ever shake." Remarkably enough, they had seldom had big gifts up until then, but from that time onwards God began to send in large sums of money.

Personal Question: Can you put your life on that same Rock?

Discussion Question: When we are on the foundation of Jesus Christ, "no man nor devil could ever shake [it]." What in your life has been shaken, what is being shaken, and what cannot be shaken? Read Hebrews 12:26–27.

2. On the fifth anniversary of the college, Rees publishes a report. Read these seven highlights from this report. On the lines underneath, write what the Lord tells you regarding your own personal circumstances.

a. "Accomplished . . . through faith and believing prayer."

_____

_____

b. "No appeal was to be made for finance."

_____

_____

c. "Visible proof that He is the living and faithful God."

_____

_____

d. "It has been the Father's will to teach us the way to trust Him each morning for the day's needs."

_____

_____

e. "The Lord has been proving us day by day that 'living faith' is above circumstances."

_____

_____

f. "The Lord allowed us to be tested beyond our strength."

_____

_____

g. "To make us rely not on ourselves."

_____

_____

Discussion Question: Read Proverbs 3:5–6. How does this passage relate to the discussion of the Bible college in this chapter?

Assignment

Write a praise paragraph, thanking the Lord for being so faithful to you in all circumstances.

_____

_____

_____

_____

_____

Chapter 27:
Buying the Second Estate

"Enlarge the place of your tent, / and let the curtains of your habitations be stretched out; / do not hold back; lengthen your cords" (Isa. 54:2). The Lord reveals to Rees that he should buy the Derwen Fawr property next. Shortly after, however, he hears that the Church of Rome wants to buy it too. This is also the time of the Great Depression, so it is not a good time to be making such a large purchase.

Discussion Question: "The Lord always shows you all the difficulties," Rees says, "when He is going to do anything through you." Can you give an example of this?

Personal Question: Rees asks for a sign from the Lord: a fifty pound check from a new source. Rees starts praising the Lord before even seeing the sign. Can you, like Rees, praise before the victory?

Read aloud:

> "All the fasting in the world is nothing to be compared with carrying liability. I would never have done it for my own family, but only for the Kingdom. The devil told me plainly that if I bought Derwen Fawr on top of

Glynderwen, I should be in the bankruptcy court. I saw myself there. But when he named the word 'bankrupt,' I also told him, 'When I was in Scotland, I said if I were to pay £10,000 for Glynderwen and the Catholics were to burn it to ashes the next day, it would still be the best investment I had ever made. So I am not only willing to be bankrupt for Derwen Fawr, but I am willing to give the last drop of my blood to save it from the Church of Rome.' The moment I said it, I came through. I felt as free as a bird in my preaching on Sunday."

We read that many vain imaginations were placed in Rees Howells' mind by the devil. It is not good to let our imaginations run away. It can cause our spirits to be depressed and not usable to God.

1. Read Romans 1:21 (KJV). What happened to their heart?

_____

_____

2. What does Rees do to the devil's arguments?

_____

_____

3. Read Second Corinthians 10:5. What are we supposed to do when the devil comes at us like this?

_____

_____

Read aloud:

> "On Monday morning I came back to Swansea and went to the agent to learn whether the negotiations had been successful. He had not come in, and while walking in the town waiting for him I met a friend who asked me where I had been over the weekend. He said he had not been able to get me out of his mind. 'No wonder!' I said, 'I have been in the bankruptcy court!' and I described the victory of Saturday night.

> "He stood for a while in thought, and then said, 'Why are you left to fight this battle alone? Are you the only Protestant in the world?'

> "'It looks like it,' I said.

> "'Well, you are not to stand alone in this,' he went on. 'If the Covenanters gave their blood to win this liberty for us, I too will give something to maintain it. Go to your agent, and if your offer is accepted come back to me for the deposit.' Victory beyond value!

> "We both stood still with tears of joy in our eyes. It had been a stiff climb, but I was able to say with Abraham, 'On the mount of the lord it shall be provided' (Gen. 22:14). And I, too, seemed to hear those words God spoke to His servant, 'Because you have done this . . . I will surely bless you . . . because you have obeyed my voice' (22:16–18). Deliverance is always found on 'the mount'; living faith must first prove to God that it has taken His word and promise for victory."

Read Psalm 111:7–8; 119:142, 151, 160.

The Word of God is trustworthy and true.

Read aloud Rees' account of "the day of climax."

In 1930, people from all around Wales gather to celebrate the dedication of Derwen Fawr. On the grounds they place a pedestal with "two scriptural statements as a permanent witness to God's faithfulness—'Jehovahjireh' and 'Faith is Substance.'"

Assignment

Write out three Bible verses on the faithfulness of God.

1. _____

_____

_____

2. _____

_____

_____

3. _____

_____

_____

Chapter 28:
Third Estate and Children's Home

Personal Question: "The Lord kept me daily and hourly abiding to fulfill the condition for claiming an answer to my prayers." Do you abide, moment by moment, in the Lord's presence?

1. Complete:

"Out of the travail came the _____ of the home and school for missionaries' children."

Discussion Question: Consider Rees' inability to purchase Sketty Park, and then the purchase of Sketty Isaf just a few weeks later. How does the hand of the Lord move before His children, both in this story and in your own life?

Read Psalm 40:1–3; Second Corinthians 4:17–18; Romans 8:18–19.

Discussion Question: Rees says, "You are always getting a death on a point that is not really essential, and then receiving a better thing for it." Do you have a personal example of having received something better after having something you thought was good taken away?

Read aloud:

> This same principle of faith was to be seen in operation on many other occasions in his life. In pursuit of some great aim which the Lord had given him he would, en route, seek and ask and believe for some particular deliverance or provision. He would obtain it, but not in the exact form in which he asked for it.
>
> To those who were watching from outside, this would often appear a failure or mistake, provoking much criticism. But the effect on him—and those on the inside with him in the battle of faith—was just the opposite; it only strengthened him in the pursuit of the main objective of faith until he had obtained it.

2. Complete:

"He would regard a temporary disappointment en route not as a failure but as a _____—rather like a climber who scales a peak mistakenly thinking it is the summit, only to find _____ and to find his _____ increased to reach it."

"Not as a failure but as a stepping stone."

3. Describe some of your recent stepping stones.

_____

_____

_____

"The Bible college at this time had about fifty students. . . . The school for missionaries' children opened in 1933, with eleven boys and girls, including some day pupils from the surrounding district who were also accepted. . . . Rees always believed the law of the hundredfold, and acted on it. He began the college with two shillings, and in fourteen years the Lord sent him £125,000."

Assignment

Read the following verses on the hundredfold and write next to each one the point or points that stand out to you.

Genesis 26:12 _____

Matthew 13:23_____

Mark 10:29–30_____

Luke 8:8 _____

Chapter 29: The Book of Common Prayer and King Edward VIII

1. What two types of prayer are mentioned?

a. _____

b. _____

Read aloud the paragraphs regarding the controversy over the new *Book of Common Prayer*, and the victory over it.

Discussion Question: What does Rees mean when he says, "The Lord had given us the victory the previous afternoon"?

"Immediately the tears became tears of joy!"

2. In 1936, King Edward VIII proposes marriage to Mrs. Wallis Simpson, a divorcée from America. The Lord leads the college to take a stand in prayer. The daily meetings' diaries from these days give an account of what happened. As you read this summary, compare it to what has happened in your life, or will happen; use it as a parallel, to know how God will respond. Write down your thoughts.

December 4. The conditions are serious. They "pleaded with the Lord to guide the king, and give wisdom."

December 5. The college has a day of prayer, and the situation is very grave.

December 6. The college has a day of prayer and fasting. "The Lord reveals that it is His will for Edward to abdicate."

December 7. "There is thanksgiving over the victory." The newspapers reveal that the king "is anxious to do only what will be best for the empire."

December 9. They trust that the Lord will help the king make the decision according to God's will.

December 10. The news of King Edward VIII's abdication becomes known. They "ask the Lord to control the country."

December 11. They "are thankful for this believing of the Holy Spirit."

_____

_____

_____

_____

_____

Discussion Question: What does the "believing of the Holy Spirit" mean?

Read aloud:

Another time Mr. Howells was needing money for the property taxes. He also knew of a man who was in the same position, and the last day had come for them both. Mr. Howells had not nearly enough for his own need, which was forty pounds, but he did have the eight pounds needed by his friend. So he went to give it to him.

When he arrived, he found the man and his wife on their knees praying for the money.

"You can get up from your knees," he said, "The Lord has told me to deliver you."

He said nothing about his own need, but on his return to the college he found a gift waiting for him—of forty pounds!

Assignment

Regarding Giving and Receiving
Read the following verses and write under them that which the Lord wants you to give forth, and what He wants to give back to you.

1. Malachi 3:8–10

Give: _____

Receive: _____

2. Luke 6:38

Give: _____

Receive: _____

3. Philippians 4:17

Give: _____

Receive: _____

Chapter 30: The Every Creature Commission

Read Psalm 139:17–18.

1. When you are in God's presence, what do you obtain?

_____

_____

_____

  2. Read Psalm 143:8–10.

a. Complete: When you are in God's presence, He teaches you to

_____.

b. Complete: God's good Spirit leads you on

_____.

c. State what the last answer means in your own words.

_____

_____

_____

Read aloud:

> On Boxing Day morning (December 26), the Spirit
> began speaking to him even earlier than usual, before he
> had arisen. Mrs. Howells, who was also awake, heard him
> repeating, "every creature, every creature."
>
> At three o'clock that morning, he was so conscious that
> God wanted to say something definite to him that he
> dressed and went to his room downstairs. There the Lord
> asked him if he believed the Savior meant His last com-
> mand to be obeyed.
>
> "I do," he replied.
>
> "Then do you believe that I can give the gospel to every
> creature?"
>
> "Without stretching a point," he answered, "I believe You
> can. You are God."
>
> "I am dwelling in you," the Lord then said. "Can I be
> responsible for this through you?"

3. Read Mark 16:15. This is the beginning of Jesus' last statement before He goes to sit at the right hand of the Father.
   Explain how important these words are.

_____

_____

_____

_____

_____

Personal Question: How do Jesus' words in Mark 16:15 pertain to you?

Someone has to obey and pray out the laborers.

Read Psalm 2:8; Matthew 9:37–38. Note the word *ask*, which is the same as *pray*.

Discussion Question: What does this word from God mean for Rees, and others who might accept the command?

4. Complete:

a. "Rees Howells came out from his room a man with a vision and a burden which never left him—the '_____

_____.'"

b. "As really as the Savior came down to the world to make

_____ for every creature, so the Holy Spirit had come down to make that atonement _____ to

_____, and that He would complete it in their generation."

Discussion Question: How do you see this being done, even now?

5. It is stated that the college becomes a "house of prayer / for all peoples" (Isa. 56:7). List the three kinds of prayer targets mentioned.

a. _____

b. _____

c. _____

6. List the kinds and varieties of prayers you think the Lord
   would have you to use in your daily devotions.

_____

_____

_____

_____

_____

This prayer warfare starts to take on different forms, one of
which is national and international intercession, specifically
concerning anything that affects world evangelism. Their
prayers are strategic, aiming to fight the devil wherever he is
"opposing freedom to evangelize." Grubb writes, "God was
preparing an instrument—a company to fight world battles
on their knees."

Discussion Question: "'Prevail against Hitler' He said to me,
and it meant three weeks of prayer and fasting." What do you
think you could obtain for national and worldwide revival by
three weeks of prayer and fasting?

The college's meeting diary records this first international
prayer battle. Read and reflect on this summary.

March 21. "We ask the Lord to deal with Germany."

March 23. "We plead with God to deal with Hitler."

March 24. The situation is "very black." "The Lord is

allowing us to plead the Every Creature Vision in His presence. The Lord turns our eyes off the countries to Himself."

Discussion Question: What is meant by the statement, "The Lord turns our eyes off the countries to Himself"?

Read aloud the account of what happens on March 29.

Personal Question: Read Ezekiel 22:30. Are you this person?

"Hitler was no more than a rod in the hands of the Holy Spirit."

7. Read Leviticus 9:22–24. Write what this passage means in your own words.

_____

_____

_____

Discussion Question: "It was essentially a clash of spiritual forces—a test of strength between the devil in Hitler and the Holy Spirit in His army of intercessors." How does this statement relate to your local and family circumstances?

Read aloud:

> At the height of the battle the one prayer that the Holy Spirit gave to the college through His servant was, "Lord, bend Hitler." A point came when that cry of travail changed in to a shout of victory. The devil had to give way.
>
> It was just before the commencement of the new session in the college, and the victory was so certain that Mr. Howells turned the opening day into a day of praise.

An announcement appeared in the *South Wales Evening Post* on Saturday, September 17, stating that "The meetings [of the following Thursday] will take the form of Praise and Thanksgiving because God has again averted a European war."

Hundreds gathered in the conference hall in that dark hour to join in praising God. In the days that followed, the test ran higher and higher, but faith was steadfast.

On Thursday, September 29, the college and school were given a general holiday to celebrate the coming victory. The next day, September 30, the Munich Agreement was signed. War had been averted!

The reason war is averted for the moment is because Hitler, for the first time, failed to obey "his Voice." "The Lord had 'bent' Hitler."

Assignment

Read Isaiah 60:14.

List some things that you would like to see bow before the Lord.

_____

_____

_____

_____

_____

Chapter 31: Ethiopia

1. Complete:

"The battle of intercession lasted for three weeks. 'It was as if we were

_____.'"

Read aloud:

> It was the first lesson for many in the college of what we have seen a number of times in Mr. Howells' life, namely: the death in an intercession which has to precede the resurrection and the test on the intercessors as to whether they can walk through their valley of humiliation, of apparent failure, with an unmoved faith.
>
> The very thing they believed for did not come to pass. The Italians were not to occupy the capital, but they did so, and the emperor was a fugitive. Rome had triumphed. It seemed the end of gospel work in the country. But Mr. Howells explained to the college a principle that he experienced throughout his life: that apparent failure may only be a stepping-stone to greater victory.

2. They are told to "walk through their valley of humiliation, of apparent failure" with what?

3. Complete:

"Apparent failure may only be a stepping-stone to _____

_____."

Read Romans 4:20–21.

When the Ethiopian emperor visits, he remarks to Mrs. Howells, "What your husband has done reminds me of an Ethiopian proverb: 'The man who has only God to look to can do all things and never fail.'"

Read Philippians 4:13 (KJV).

"God's answer was perfect."

Read Psalm 20:4–7. Discuss this passage verse by verse.

Assignment

Write some of the perfections of God that appeal to you.

_____

_____

_____

_____

_____

Remember, you are His offspring.

Chapter 32: Visitation of the Spirit

After the dedication on March 29, 1936, the college begins to change. The Spirit is at work, and the staff and students start to lay "their lives on the altar as intercessors." Grubb compares this time in the college to the Pentecost. They are not merely a group of individuals working towards a common goal, but "a body in the full sense of the term—a living, integrated organism, infused with one life and one purpose."

1. Read Genesis 8:20.

Complete: The altar is a place of _____.

2. Read Exodus 30:1, 7–8.

Complete: The altar is a place for _____.

3. Read Exodus 29:12.

Complete: The altar is a place where the _____ is applied.

4. Read Leviticus 6:13.

Complete: The fire must be kept burning on the altar _____

_____.

Read Romans 15:6.

Discussion Question: Rees says, "There was an increasing consciousness of God's presence. . . . They wept before Him for hours—broken at the corruption of their own hearts revealed in the light of His holiness." Discuss what the holiness of God means to you.

5. Look up *holiness of God* in a Bible dictionary.

_____

_____

6. Look up *holiness of man* in a Bible dictionary.

_____

_____

7. Read First Peter 1:16; Revelation 4:8. Why does God want His children to be holy?

_____

_____

_____

Read aloud Rees' description of how the Holy Spirit came, and how it affected them.

Personal Question: Dr. Kingsley C. Priddy says, "The person of the Holy Spirit filled all our thoughts . . . His light seemed to penetrate all the hidden recesses of our hearts." Have you felt like this recently?

8. Complete:

a. "It was not so much _____ we saw as _____.

We saw _____and _____

underlying everything we had ever done. _____ and

_____were discovered in places where we

had never suspected them."

b. "In His nature He [the Holy Spirit] was just like _____

—He would never_____ but always

_____."

> ## "There is all the difference in the world between *your* surrendered life in My hands, and Me living *My* life in your body."

As they read the book of Acts in a new light, they realize that they are reading the acts of the Holy Spirit, not the acts of the apostles. Rees says, "The Holy Spirit as a divine person lived in the bodies of the apostles, even as the Savior had lived His earthly life in the body that was born in Bethlehem. And all that the Holy Spirit asked of us was our wills and our bodies."

9. For each verse, list the person that is indwelt by the Holy Spirit.

a. Acts 4:8 _____

b. Acts 7:55 _____

c. Acts 13:9 _____

10. Complete:

"And all that the Holy Spirit asked of us was our _____
and our _____."

Read Romans 12:1. Discuss Dr. Priddy's comments on this verse.

"How much there was in us that still wanted to live our own lives!"

11. Read Luke 9:24. Rewrite this verse in your own words, as it pertains to you.

_____

_____

_____

"Why had He manifested Himself to us in this way? He made that quite clear. It was because there was a work to be done in the world today that only He [the Holy Spirit] could do."

12. Read John 16:8. What does the Holy Spirit convict people of?

_____

_____

_____

Discussion Question: The Holy Spirit says, "You will find all that you need in Jesus. But I have come to put you to the cross, so that I may live in your body for the sake of a lost world."

Read Colossians 3:3; Second Corinthians 4:10; Galatians 2:20. What do this quote and these verses mean to you personally?

13. Complete:

a. "'_____' would never be able to hold out."

b. "The final contest between _____ and _____ for the kingdoms of _____ _____."

c. "We could see only one person who was '_____ for these things' (2 Cor. 2:16), and He was the glorious _____ _____ of the Godhead in those whom He was able to indwell."

Personal Question: Are you that person "in whom He [is] able to indwell"?

Discussion Question: How does all this relate to what is going on in the Christian and non-Christian world right now?

Discussion Question: What does Rees mean by "bringing our experience up to the level of His Word"?

Read aloud:

"But far greater than anything His visitation could mean to us personally was what it was going to mean to the world. We saw Him as the One to whom 'the nations are like a drop from a bucket, / and are accounted as the dust

on the scales' (Isa. 40:15). On our faces before Him we
could only say, from awed hearts, 'Holy Spirit, You have
come to shake the world.'"

Personal Question: Read Isaiah 2:19; 13:13; Ezekiel 38:20;
Joel 3:16; Haggai 2:6–7; Hebrews 12:26. Are you becoming
one that cannot be shaken?

"We also recognize His mighty working in and through others."

The Holy Spirit is going to fulfill prophesy
"through His prepared channels, in all parts of
the world."

"One body for one God-appointed purpose—and this was
now one of them."

Assignment

Look up the word *shake* in a variety of dictionaries and list
the meanings here.

_____

_____

_____

_____

_____

Chapter 33:
Fourth Estate and the Jews

As we look back at the college's years of intercession for Israel, it is amazing to see the answers to their prayers. But at the time, there did not seem to be any visible signs that their prayers would be fulfilled. Grubb writes, "It reminds us that no great event in history, even though prophesied beforehand in the Scriptures, comes to pass unless God finds His human channels of faith and obedience."

"I firmly believe the times of the Gentiles are drawing to a close, and the Jews must be back in their own land when the Master returns." Read Luke 21:24.

1. Look up the word *Gentile*.

_____

_____

Read Jeremiah 16:15.

The Lord tells Rees to "make a home" for the thousands of Jewish refugee children. He whispers the name "Penllergaer" to Rees, and for the next few weeks Rees prays constantly. On

November 26, he declares that he will buy the estate. And, he says, "I am willing to risk my all in order to help the Jews."

> **"Unless He in you makes the suffering your own, you can't intercede for them. You will never touch the Throne. Unless you send up that real cry; words don't count at all."**

Read First Thessalonians 5:16–18.

2. Whom does Rees Howells say he has to look to, to be his Company?

_____

Discussion Question: Grubb writes that God "had His army of the Spirit." What does this mean in the context of this chapter? Read Ephesians 6:12; Joel 2:11; 3:9. What do these passages say about this army?

Read Exodus 19:5–6.

3. Look up the word *covenant*.

_____

_____

The college prays that, because of God's covenant with Abraham, God will take His people back to their land, and that Palestine will again become a Jewish State. They devote this to prayer for weeks, but they receive word that "the partitioning of Palestine had not been carried." Instead of losing faith, this only spurs them on to more intense prayer. They see "God's angels influencing those men in the United Nations Conference in New York to work on behalf of God's people." Before they even hear the news about the United Nations' vote, they "had full assurance of victory."

"The State of Israel was a fact."

Read aloud Rees' telling of what the Lord reveals to him concerning the Arabs.

Assignment

What do you think is God's covenant with you?

_____

_____

_____

_____

_____

As you read the Bible daily, keep this covenant in mind when you come across the promises of God.

Chapter 34:
Intercession for Dunkirk

Throughout the course of World War II, the Lord changes Rees' burden from local issues to national and international concerns. In reflecting on this time he says, "The world became our parish and we were led to be responsible to intercede for countries and nations."

Discussion Question: Rees sees that the devil is using Hitler to try to prevent the gospel from "going to every creature." How is that still true now, regarding Satan's agents?

1. In 1939 Rees writes a book called *God Challenges the Dictators: Doom of Nazis Predicted*. In this book, what dynamic prophetic statement does Rees make regarding Stalin?

_____

_____

_____

2. Complete:

We "have to cry out to God in our _____ for the _____ which will certainly come."

Read aloud:

> In spite of this apparent setback . . . we find ourselves certainly not among a fearful company—nor even chiefly among a praying one—but rather among those who are already on victory ground, when people's hearts are failing them for fear all around. And what gave them such clarity and assurance that theirs was the victory? The outward "death" of the prediction!

> If we say God was not with them, we may well ask ourselves this question: "Was there anywhere else in the whole of Britain, America or elsewhere among God's people another such company, maybe a hundred strong, who were on their knees day by day holding fast the victory by faith—while soldiers across the water were retreating mile by mile, whole countries surrendering and the enemy within sight of their goal?"

> From this time on, through all the years of the war the whole college was in prayer every evening from seven o'clock to midnight with only a brief interval for supper. They never missed a day. This was in addition to an hour's prayer meeting every morning, and very often at midday. There were many special periods when every day was given up wholly to prayer and fasting.

> In the meetings just before Whitsunday Mr. Howells said:

> "Through God we made the prediction; through God we stand to it; and through God we are going against the enemy. He tells me tonight, 'Don't you fear because of that prediction you sent out; don't you fear the Nazis.' I think what a glory it is that we don't need to change our prayers

one bit, in spite of the present developments. I am so glad that it has been the Kingdom we have had before us all the time in the last nine months, and I haven't a single regret. The Lord has said, 'I am going to deal with the Nazis.' It has been a battle between the Holy Spirit and the devil which we have been fighting for four years."

Read aloud:

On Whitsunday, when instead of peace having been declared, Hitler only two days before had invaded Holland and Belgium, Rees Howells spoke at the college meeting.

"We shall never defend the prediction. The point is: Can God put a doubt in us who have really believed? If God tells you that this delay is for His glory, then you must take victory in it. There is no glory in delay, unless there was faith to put it through. I would be a different man today if there was failure, but the Holy Spirit is not a failure. I can really thank Him for the delay. I wouldn't be without this experience for the world. Very strange that what is death in the eyes of the world is victory to the Holy Spirit."

"Death in the eyes of the world is victory to the Holy Spirit."

Read First Corinthians 15:36; John 12:24; First Peter 1:23.

"The Lord has made very plain that the victory is from Him and no one else, and He is to have all the glory."

3. Complete:

"God gets at the enemy _____ and _____."

Discussion Question: What does this mean?

Read and reflect on the meeting notes from May 17. Discuss Rees' comments on the previous night's victory.

Discussion Question: Rees says, "The delay has not changed our faith a bit. . . . Christianity is quite safe." What do you think he means by this?

"If you have faith, you can leave it in His hand, and He will intervene in the right time."

4. Grubb writes, "As the Nazis poured through Europe, the college stood daily before God." Read and reflect on these short statements from Rees' messages during this period. Consider how they may relate to your life and write a short personal comment.

a. "You do not know how much faith is needed."

_____

_____

b. "Our eyes are on Him today."

_____

_____

c. "Unless He intervenes, we are lost."

_____

_____

d. "Man would not be able to end this."

_____

_____

e. "Don't expect Me to do it until you get to your extremity."

_____

_____

f. "In the darkest hour."

_____

_____

5. What is the only reason they are not in a panic on May 22?

_____

_____

_____

6. What do they have to do until God does the "big thing"?

_____

_____

_____

Discussion Question: How do they keep the enemy in check? How can we keep the Enemy in check?

Personal Question: "All you can do today when a cry will go up from the country is to be in a position to take the answer from God." Can you take the answer?

Discussion Question: On the day of the evacuation of Dunkirk, Rees says, "The battle is the Holy Spirit's. See Him outside yourselves tonight; He is there on the battlefield with His drawn sword." Read this statement aloud, then close your eyes and visualize what it means. What meaning have you come up with and what have you seen?

Read aloud the college's notes from May 30 and Grubb's paragraph of reflections on those years.

**"God had this company of hidden interces-
sors whose lives were on the altar day after day
as they stood in the gap for the deliverance of
Britain."**

Assignment

List some of the intercessions God has assigned to you.

1. _____

2. _____

3. _____

4. _____

5. _____

6. _____

7. _____

Chapter 35: The Battle of Britain

Read aloud:

> "Must we have fear because others have fear? If I trusted God to bring these properties into being, I am going to trust God to protect them. I want you to get a foundation for this trust. We need a real foundation for our faith, in case the raids will last for months. Can we trust Him for the impossible in this, the same as in finance?"

1. Must you have fear because others have fear?

_____

_____

_____

2. Can we trust Him for the impossible?

_____

_____

_____

3. What is the only thing Rees fears?

_____

Discussion Question: Read Joshua 1:5; Psalm 57:1. What do these passages say about fear?

Discussion Question: Read the journal notes from the time of the air raids (September 2, 3, 4, and 7). What can you learn from Rees' reflections about fear and about God's protection?

"This peace the Savior gives is not an artificial one. It is so deep that even the devil can't disturb it."

"You can't take a shade of fear into the presence of God."

Read Isaiah 8:11–13; John 14:27; Philippians 4:7.

Read aloud:

> It was at this point that the burden of prayer for protection and the questionings of the past few days changed into praise and certainty.

> Full assurance of victory was given, and it rings out in Rees Howells' words, "What victory! Those who are in the Spirit see it as victory, because He has found believing in us. What joy! What praise! God would probably not give faith for victory in the war until personal victory was first gained." The all-clear sounded as the service finished.

> They sang in closing, "Death is vanquished! Tell it with joy, ye faithful."[1]

Read Second Timothy 1:12.

Discussion Question: What does Rees mean when he says, "How could we get victory for the world unless we had first believed it for ourselves?"

4. Complete:

a. "The Holy Spirit has found _____ equal to what He wants to do."

b. "Take care you are _____.
Believing is the most delicate thing you can think of. It is like a _____."

c. "He couldn't do it before without _____."

"When you believe, you finish with prayer."

Talk about the delicate vapor of what your "believing" is.

Read aloud the college's notes from September 12.

5. Complete: List the three things they believe will come to pass, as found in the college's notes from September 14.

a. _____

b. _____

c. _____

Read aloud the events of September 15, beginning with Churchill's *War Memoirs*.

Assignment

Explain how the power of God is able to be released onto this earth.

_____

_____

_____

_____

_____

1. Crosby, Fanny. "Praise Him, Praise Him," accessed April 21, 2016, http://www.hymntime.com/tch/htm/p/h/i/phimphim.htm.

Chapter 36:
Russia, North Africa, Italy, D-Day

One of the college's main prayers is that the Lord will bring Russia into the war to "deal with Communism." Weeks later, Russia does come into the war. But shortly after, Russia is in danger of collapsing. As Hitler's armies approach Moscow, the Lord begins to speak to Rees. He tells him to pray and believe for Him to "save Moscow and give a setback to the Nazis." To some in the college, this seems impossible, as it appears that Moscow's fall is inevitable.

Discussion Question: Dr. Kenneth G. Symonds says, "But although the prayer was so far beyond us, yet the Spirit laid it on us." What does this mean?

1. When Moscow does not fall, the Lord begins to turn the college's prayer in another direction. Where are their prayers now to be centered?

_____

2. The Lord reveals that three things will happen through the war. What are they?

a. _____

b. _____

c. _____

North Africa is the next area of immediate danger. If Egypt falls, then "the door was wide open to Palestine." If God does not intervene, Palestine will not be a safe place for the Jews.

3. Complete:

"These Bible Lands must be protected, because it is to these lands

_____."

Rees says to the Lord, "Unless there is a special reason for Egypt to fall, don't let Alexandria be taken, but give Rommel a setback." The college is called to spend Saturday afternoon in prayer about this. Rees says to them, "Is this prayer of the Holy Spirit? If it is, we can be as sure of the enemy not taking Alexandria as the people will be when they hear it." The next evening, Rees and the college "come through to victory." They know that Rommel will never take Egypt.

Read aloud the story of Major Rainier and the battle for Alexandria.

Regarding this events of the battle for Alexandria, a magazine editor wrote, "The hand of Almighty God is in evidence once more, coming to our aid when weighty issues are in the balance." Read Ezra 8:31; First Peter 5:6–7.

Discussion Question: How is God's hand even now on you, your family, and the nations?

4. After Alexandria, what is the next triumph of the Holy Spirit? How does the college react when the news gets dark and believing that the Spirit will prevail seems to go against human reason?

_____

_____

_____

"We found the enemy was giving way before us."

Personal Question: What has to be done in your life in order for God to be able to pray through you like He does through those in the college?

Read Joel 2:12–13.

Prayer: *Lord, purge my heart of all uncleanness. Show me Your will and Your way. Make my paths straight. In Jesus' name, Amen.*

Read aloud Dr. Symonds telling of "the day of the landing at Salerno."

"This only served to confirm to us the guidance of the Spirit." Read John 16:13; First Corinthians 2:10–13.

Discussion Question: Rees says, "We have a perfect right to ask God to come and fight with our young men." Why did they have a "right" to ask God to do this?

5. How was the establishment of the United Nations an answer to years of prayer?

_____

_____

_____

Assignment

List the things you are doing or will do so that every creature might hear the gospel.

_____

_____

_____

_____

_____

Chapter 37: Home Call

"This period of intercession was now ended. During the war years, God had called the college apart to intercede for the world—as years before He had shut in Rees Howells alone with Himself to intercede for one soul."

1. Now that the war is over, where does the college shift their focus? What does that look like for them?

_____

_____

_____

Read aloud:

> The special burden on Mr. Howells' own heart was finance for getting the gospel to every creature—finance which could be expended freely in the support of God's servants in all lands. This burden never left him until Sunday, January 15, 1950. In the nine o'clock meeting that night he read the songs of Moses and David; then he said, "Everything in me is praising God because the Holy Spirit can say, 'I glorified you on earth, having accomplished the work that you have me to do' (John 17:4). Every creature will hear the gospel, the finance for the vision is safe and the King will come back."

He had the assurance that God would give the promised £100,000, which he would then invest in His work and claim the hundredfold for fulfilling the Every Creature Commission.

2. Complete:

"The Holy Spirit would _____ in the future to overcome _____ and reach every creature with the gospel in _____ _____."

3. After his first heart attack, why does Rees refuse rest and medication?

_____

_____

_____

Personal Question: Rees Howells "had been faithful in the hands of God in laying the foundation." Have you been faithful in doing what God has asked you to do?

"[The] college and school had the same Guide,
Enabler and Supplier—the Lord Himself."

Read aloud the events of Rees' final days, from the February 8 meeting to the end of the chapter.

Discussion Question: What allows the marvelous presence of God to be present at the departure of a godly man?

Assignment

Read the following verses and answer the questions regarding life and death. If this is your last session, do this assignment aloud with the group.

1. Read Ephesians 6:11–12. Who is the enemy of life?

_____

2. Read Luke 13:16. Who keeps people in bondage?

_____

3. Read John 8:44.

Complete: The devil is a _____ and a

_____.

4. Read John 3:16. What do we receive from Jesus?

_____

5. Read Hebrews 2:14–15. Jesus became human and died that He might do what two things?

a. _____

b. _____

6. Read Second Timothy 1:10. What has the appearance of Jesus abolished? What has it brought to light?

_____

_____

Conclusion

Discussion Question: What stands out most to you in this whole study?

Discussion Question: How has this study affected your relationship to God?

Discussion Question: After completing this study, what changes will you make in your life? What goals will you establish? What new direction will your life take?

PUBLICATIONS

Fort Washington, PA 19034

This book is published by CLC Publications, an outreach of CLC Ministries International. The purpose of CLC is to make evangelical Christian literature available to all nations so that people may come to faith and maturity in the Lord Jesus Christ. We hope this book has been life changing and has enriched your walk with God through the work of the Holy Spirit. If you would like to know more about CLC, we invite you to visit our website:
www.clcusa.org

To know more about the remarkable story of the founding of CLC International we encourage you to read

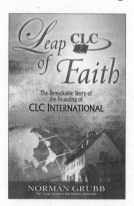

LEAP OF FAITH

Norman Grubb

Paperback
Size 5¹/₄ x 8, Pages 248
ISBN: 978-0-87508-650-7
ISBN (*e-book*): 978-1-61958-055-8